实用英汉翻译教程

A Practical English-Chinese Translation Course

周守晋 编著

图书在版编目(CIP)数据

实用英汉翻译教程 / 周守晋编著 —北京:北京大学出版社,2017.1

ISBN 978-7-301-27716-4

Ⅰ.①实… Ⅱ.①周… Ⅲ.①英语—翻译—教材 Ⅳ.①H315.9

中国版本图书馆 CIP 数据核字(2016)第 266815 号

书　　　名	实用英汉翻译教程 SHIYONG YING-HAN FANYI JIAOCHENG
著作责任者	周守晋　编著
责 任 编 辑	李　凌
标 准 书 号	ISBN 978-7-301-27716-4
出 版 发 行	北京大学出版社
地　　　址	北京市海淀区成府路 205 号　100871
网　　　址	http://www.pup.cn　新浪微博:@北京大学出版社
电 子 信 箱	zpup@pup.cn
电　　　话	邮购部 62752015　发行部 62750672　编辑部 62753027
印 刷 者	北京大学印刷厂
经 销 者	新华书店 787 毫米×1092 毫米　16 开本　14 印张　275 千字 2017 年 1 月第 1 版　2017 年 1 月第 1 次印刷
定　　　价	39.00 元

未经许可,不得以任何方式复制或抄袭本书之部分或全部内容。
版权所有,侵权必究
举报电话:010-62752024　电子信箱:fd@pup.pku.edu.cn
图书如有印装质量问题,请与出版部联系,电话:010-62756370

目 录
CONTENTS

致　谢
Acknowledgements ……………………………………………………………… 1
编写说明
About This Book ………………………………………………………………… 3
英汉语言比较
Comparison Between Chinese and English …………………………………… 7
英汉翻译方法简介
A Brief Introduction to English-Chinese Translation Methods ……………… 15
标点符号用法示例
Examples about Punctuation Marks …………………………………………… 20

第一单元　说明文
Unit 1　Exposition

第 一 课　为什么学外语
　　　　　Reasons for Studying a Foreign Language ………………………… 3
第 二 课　中国古代科技及其影响
　　　　　Science and China's Influence on the World ……………………… 12
第 三 课　女性成功的秘密
　　　　　Ten Power Tips: What Are the Real Secrets of Success? ………… 20
第 四 课　运动快餐计划
　　　　　An "Exercise Snack" Plan ………………………………………… 30

第二单元　记叙文
Unit 2　Narration

第 五 课　叱咤风云
　　　　　The Man of the Moment …………………………………………… 43
第 六 课　要做真正的美国人
　　　　　The Struggle to Be an All American Girl ………………………… 55

第 七 课　冰雪不归路
　　　　　An Arduous and Determined Trek ………………………………………… 66

第三单元　议论文
Unit 3　Argumentation

第 八 课　如何看待中国的影响力
　　　　　Tempered View of China's Might …………………………………………… 77

第 九 课　学会成功
　　　　　Learning to Succeed ………………………………………………………… 85

第 十 课　亚洲的变化
　　　　　Changes in Asia ……………………………………………………………… 94

第四单元　应用文
Unit 4　Practical Writing

第十一课　招生、就业与住房
　　　　　Admission, Employment and Residential ………………………………… 111

第十二课　休闲与娱乐
　　　　　Leisure and Entertainment ………………………………………………… 127

附　　录
Appendix

附录1:部分课后练习参考答案

Appendix I: Keys to Some Parts of Main Text Exercises ……………………………… 141

附录2:补充材料参考译文及部分练习答案

Appendix II: Sample Translations of the Supplementary Materials and Keys
　　　　　to Some Parts of Supplementary Exercises ……………………………… 153

附录3:翻译练习

Appendix III: Translation Exercises ……………………………………………………… 173

附录4:翻译练习参考答案

Appendix IV: Keys to the Translation Exercises ……………………………………… 181

附录5:译作选登

Appendix V: Selected Sample Translation Papers …………………………………… 184

致 谢
Acknowledgements

感谢以下作者及机构授权使用相关材料。

We are grateful to the following authors and institutions for granting the permission to use their property right works in this book.

Andrew Hill, Tempered View of China's Might, *Financial Times*, UK, Nov. 1, 2006.

Angela Gallagher-Brett, Reasons for Studying a Foreign Language, *700 Reasons for Studying Languages*, www.llas.ac.uk/700reasons.

Colin A. Ronan, The Shorter Science and Civilization in China, *An Abridgement of Joseph Needham's Original Text*, Cambridge University Press, UK, 1978.

Ian McMorran (麦穆伦), My Life in China, *Chinese version is in Oriental Outlook* (Weekly), PRC 2007 10th Issue.

John Pickrell, Tea Boosts Immunity and Helps Skin, National Geographic News, *National Geography*, USA, Apr. 29, 2003.

Jos W. Becker, Changes in Asia, *World Culture Report 2000*, UNESCO Press, 2000.

Julie Scelfo, Ten Powerful Tips: What are the Real Secrets of Success, *Newsweek*, USA, Sep. 25, 2006 Issue.

Li Li, Outstanding Rocker in China: Cui Jian, *Beijing Review* (Weekly), PRC, Dec. 21, 2006.

Paul Eccleston, Times Atlas Shows Effect of Global Warming, *Daily Telegraph*, UK, Sep. 3, 2007.

Robert M. Worcester, Changing Roles of Women in Europe, *World Culture Report 2000*, UNESCO Press, 2000.

Wu jiao, Pressure of Work Takes Its Toll, *China Daily*, PRC, Feb. 5, 2007.

Yang Cheng, Sino-EU Partnership Touches New High, *China Daily*, PRC, May 9, 2007.

编写说明
About This Book

1. 学习者/使用者

　　本教材为具有中级以上汉语水平，希望学习和提高英汉翻译技能、或者通过英汉翻译练习进一步提高汉语水平的学习者编写。就汉语水平而言，学习者应该初步掌握了汉语的基本语法，学习了2000—3000个常用词语；就翻译水平而言，应初步具备了就熟悉的话题进行简短口译和笔译的能力。

　　学习英汉翻译，需要有良好的英语基础；不过这并不意味着学习者的母语或者第一语言必须是英语。实际上，很多母语为非英语的同学，在英汉翻译这门课上同样取得了很好的成绩。

　　在教学实践中我们发现，学习者的情况千差万别，比如达到中级以上水平所需要的时间不同；同是中级以上水平的学习者，在词汇、语法、汉字识读和书写等能力上存在着差异；即使是同一个学习者，在口头表达和书面表达的能力上也可能有所不同。另一方面，学习者的需求也不尽相同。有的学习者希望通过"英汉翻译"课程的学习，比较系统地掌握翻译的方法和技巧；有的学习者则希望通过英汉语言的比较，达到对汉语更加全面、深入的认识，提高汉语表达的能力。

　　本书作为一本短期强化、强调实用的语言技能训练教材，我们希望在明确针对性的同时，在知识—技能、语言—文化、系统性—灵活性等方面取得平衡。相应的，我们鼓励学习者根据自己的条件和需求，灵活地使用本教材。比如，起步阶段的学习者可以按照课文、词语练习、翻译方法举例、语法练习和改错的顺序开展学习，打下比较扎实的基础；水平较高的学习者则可以以译句分析、词语翻译为重点，加强翻译技能、提高文化认知和跨文化交际能力，同时也可以对参考译文进行评析（critical reading）；有扎实汉语基础的学习者（比如汉语口语水平较高的华裔学生），则可以重点学习翻译方法，通过翻译练习系统强化汉语语法和书面表达的知识、技能。

　　使用这本教材的教师也可以根据实际条件和需要，对讲授内容、练习方式、讨论范围、教学进度等进行灵活安排，比如可以安排"每日/周一练"，根据实际情况，发挥自己的优势，选择满足学生需求、内容不断更新的材料开展讲练；还可以由学生自己选择材料，主持讲练或展开讨论；在"改错"环节，教师完全可以选择所教学生的练习中实际出现的问题进行讲解或讨论。

总之，这本教材提供了一个观念、方法的参考框架，使用者可以根据自己的情况进行取舍、改造，使得学生在学习这门课时更具主动性、创造性，让英汉翻译的课堂充满活力，提高学习效率。

2. 教学/学习目标

这本教材旨在帮助学习者达到以下三个目标：

(1) 能翻译（以英译汉为主）报纸杂志上的一般文章或较为通俗的专业文章（有时需借助工具书），内容准确、语句通顺。

(2) 通过英—汉语言比较和翻译练习，扩大汉语的词汇量、提高表达的准确性、丰富性，对汉语语法、表达习惯具有更加深入的认识。

(3) 丰富对英—汉两种语言在思维方式、文化特征上共性与差异的认识，提高跨文化交际的能力。

为了达到上述目标，我们在教学内容、材料、方法和练习等方面进行了相应的探索，主要是：

(1) 选材内容广泛，覆盖语言、文化、历史、社会、教育、商业、城市、环境、健康、休闲、娱乐等二十多个主题。学习者既可以了解不同领域的文章在词语、内容等方面对翻译提出的要求，也可以逐渐掌握不同文体、不同语言风格材料的翻译方法。

(2) 围绕两条主线组织课文和展开教学。一条主线是循序渐进地介绍英汉翻译的基本方法，结合课文语言材料展开相应的练习。另一条主线是从词、短语的对应到句段、篇章的翻译，逐步加深对英、汉语言结构规律的认识，促进翻译能力的提高。

(3) 设置了多种形式的练习。有针对材料内容的理解—思考型练习，针对具体观点、信息的讨论—表达型练习，针对翻译方法的词—句转换型练习，针对翻译能力提高的结构—篇章转换型练习，针对语言/文化比较的判断—改错型练习。这些不同形式的练习，核心是体现翻译基本要求的不同方面和层次，反映翻译过程各个环节的规律和要求。

以上的考虑和安排，根本目的是给学习者打下一个比较扎实的基础、促进其自主学习的意识和能力的增强，切实提高其翻译水平。

3. 教材的结构

这本教材以单元为框架，包括：说明文单元（第 1—4 课）、记叙文单元（第 5—7 课）、议论文单元（第 8—10 课）、应用文单元（11—12 课）。"单元教学"是现代外语教学发展的趋势之一，能够较好地体现语言的功能特点和语言的使用特点，有利于满足教学的系统性、针对性要求。

从英汉翻译课来看，教学的目标之一是使学习者掌握方法（既包括英汉翻译的技能、方法，也包括语言、文化比较和理解的方法）。书面表达的选词、造句、修辞以及篇章语体等方面，都要受文体的制约；因此，以单元（文体）为本进行翻译教学，有利于学生全面、准确地理解和掌握方法，把握学习的基本内容及其相互关联。

从翻译方法和语言技能训练来看，教材的四个单元各有侧重：第一单元以基本句型的翻译训练为中心，强调语序、名词、动词和形容词的翻译；第二单元以句子关系和时间表达为中心；第三单元的中心是复杂的句子结构、短语的翻译训练；第四单元的中心是"措辞"（词语和表达格式的选择）和语体风格训练。当然，这些分工不必绝对化，单元之间教学重点的安排可以有所调整、交替甚至部分重复，以加深对学习内容的理解和掌握、促进某些重要技能的掌握。

每篇课文主要由三部分构成：(1) 课文以及对课文相关内容（词语、结构、表达和文化）的讲解、练习；(2) 有针对性的（与课文内容或教学目的相关的知识、技能）训练与讨论；(3) 总结、提高性的讨论和练习。具体编排如下：

- ☐ 课文——主题明确，内容丰富，长短、难度适宜并包含相应"语言点"。
- ☐ 解题——对课文相关内容、本课学习重点进行简要说明。
- ☐ 词语注释——主要是对学生难以把握的词语和表达进行简单解释，提供选择。
- ☐ 根据课文内容回答问题——用汉语概括相关内容、提炼主旨大意，开展相关讨论。
- ☐ 词语翻译练习——把握英、汉词语在构成、意义、使用上的异同。
- ☐ 翻译方法——简要讲解基本翻译方法，开展相关训练。
- ☐ 语法练习——针对英—汉翻译结构转换上的难点、重点进行讲解、练习。
- ☐ 指出并改正译句中的错误——通过纠正错误，提高选词、造句的能力。
- ☐ 讨论——拓展翻译学习的过程，实现翻译→交际的转换，体现翻译的意义。

课文材料和各类练习/讨论材料，是根据内容与形式兼备、代表性与多样性共存以及体现教育意义、趣味性和实用性等原则，对中外英文报刊、图书等载体上的文章进行摘录、改编。话题涉及社会、历史、文化、政治、经济、教育、科技、商贸以及日常生活等不同的领域,对于学习者开阔视野、激发学习兴趣、扩大词汇量、提高翻译技巧和能力具有促进作用,对于学习者了解东、西方文化的共性与差异也有积极的作用。

4．教学时间

本教材可供一个学期（约 15 周）教学使用,每周可安排 4—6 课时,总共 60—90 课时,即每单元的教学时间是 15—23 小时。各个单元之间可以根据课文数量、教学或学生学习情况的不同,在时间上进行适当调剂。教师也可以根据实际情况,对教材内容进行适当增删,以更好地满足教学需要。这里结合我们的教学实践,内容和时间的安排建议如下:

周学时 学习时限	2 学时/周	4 学时/周	6 学时/周
一个学期 （约 15 周）	共 30 学时。围绕主课文材料,基本解决词、句翻译问题。	共 60 学时。在课文词句翻译的基础上,增加补充材料,进行语言对比和翻译方法训练。	共 90 学时。全面使用教材提供的材料,充分开展各项学习和训练。
一个学年 （约 30 周）	共 60 学时。在课文词句翻译的基础上,增加补充材料,进行语言对比和翻译方法训练。	共 120 学时。在完成教材教学内容的基础上,扩大补充材料,增加练习分量。	共 180 学时。在教材框架基础上,增加汉译英、口译、篇章综合翻译训练。

英 汉 语 言 比 较
Comparison Between Chinese and English

学习外语，翻译是有效的方法之一。翻译可以使我们了解不同语言之间的差异和共性，发现规律，提高学习的效率。翻译也可以帮助我们找到差异的原因，发现语言里的社会—文化内容，加深对一种外语（或是第二、第三语言）和它所代表的文化的认识，从而更好地掌握这种语言。

反过来看，对两种语言的差异和共性有一定的认识，又是开展翻译的必要条件；对于语言差异和共性的了解越广泛、越具体，翻译的质量就会越高。可见，外语学习、翻译、语言比较存在着相互促进的关系，三者构成一个你中有我、我中有你、难以截然分开的整体。

比较英—汉语言的异同，可以从不同的角度入手。下面主要从英—汉翻译的角度，结合许多同行专家的研究成果，简要说明两种语言在结构、词汇、表达习惯和相应的文化背景方面一些相同和不同之处。

1. 英汉句子结构的比较

结构是句子的组织形式。为了说明一件事情，句子一般有主语（subject）、谓语（predicate）和宾语（object）。比如：

① He   bought   a new pair of shoes.
　　他　　　买了　　　一双新鞋子。
　　主语　　谓语　　　宾语

这个句子说明"谁—做了—什么"（Who did what），英、汉句子的结构和语序基本相同。但是，除了说明"谁做了什么"，句子经常还要说明"怎么（做）""为什么（做）"等情况。例如：

② He bought a new pair of shoes.
　 He bought himself a new pair of shoes.
　 He bought himself a new pair of shoes at SMG.
　 He bought himself a new pair of shoes at SMG yesterday.
　 He bought himself a new pair of shoes at SMG yesterday in order to meet the girl.

He bought himself a new pair of shoes at SMG yesterday in order to meet the girl he loved.

他买了一双新鞋子。

他给自己买了一双新鞋子。

他在SMG给自己买了一双新鞋子。

昨天他在SMG给自己买了一双新鞋子。

为了跟那个姑娘见面，昨天他在SMG给自己买了一双新鞋子。

为了跟他喜欢的那个姑娘见面，昨天他在SMG给自己买了一双新鞋子。

可见，当增加新信息的时候，英语的结构倾向于向右发展（Right Branching Direction，or RBD），汉语的结构则倾向于向左发展（Left Branching Direction，or LBD）。再看下面这首英国儿歌：

③ That is the malt

　　that lay in the house that Jack built

　This is the rat

　　that ate the malt

　　that lay in the house that Jack built

变成句子就是：

④ This is the rat that ate the malt that lay in the house that Jack built.
　　①　　　②　　　③　　　　　④　　　　　⑤
　　这是　吃了　放在杰克盖的房子里的麦芽糖　的　那只老鼠
　　①　　　　　③＋⑤＋④　　　　　　　　　　②

RBD与LBD的不同，说明英、汉句子表达意义的方式存在差异。例如表示存在（existential）的意义，英语、汉语的表达方式分别是：

英语：存在（existential there V）＋ 存在的东西 ＋ 地方/时间
汉语：地方/时间 ＋ 存在（existential there V）＋ 存在的东西

例如：

⑤ There is a dangerous intersection at one end of the block. Before a stop sign was put up, there were ninety accidents there in a year.

街区的尽头有一个危险的路口，在禁行标志竖起之前，一年中有九十起事故。

⑥ Where there is a hope, there is a way.

哪里有希望，哪里就有路（即：有志者事竟成）。

再例如，英语的it形式主语句，在意义上相当于汉语的话题句：

⑦ It is offensive to make such comparison.
做这种比较是令人不快的。

⑧ It was far-sighted of her to buy up that property.
她买下那笔财产真是有远见。

⑨ It is not woman's exclusive duty to take care of the children.
照顾孩子并非是妇女专有的义务。

英语用 it 作形式主语，真正的主语放在后面（右边），汉语则要把主语放在前面（左边），作为句子的话题。

汉语的"把"字句，也与向左发展的结构有关。比较下面的句子：

⑩ I parked my car there. ＝I parked my car,（that caused）the car parked there.
我把车停在那儿了。＝我停车,（使得）车停在那儿了。

这种包含使役结构（causative construction）的句子可以分析为：

主语［subject/causer］＋动词［transitive & causative］＋宾语［objective］＋补语［complement］

　　I　　　　　　　　　parked　　　　　　　　　　　　　my car
→ I parked my car（the action），my car is there（the result）
　　我　　停车，车停在那儿了
→ 我　把车　停在那儿了

在"把"字句里，宾语既是受事（the patient of an action），又是结果部分的主语（the subject of the result）。为了强调宾语的这种特点，汉语用介词（preposition.）"把"来标记（mark）宾语，同时把它放在动词的前面（左边）：

　　太阳　融（化）雪，　雪（融）化　了
→ 　太阳　把雪　融化了
　　他关门，门关上了
→ 　他　把门　关上了

2. 英汉词语比较

词语有形式（form）、意义（meaning）和用法（usage）等方面。英、汉词语在这些方面既有相似的地方，也存在着很大的差异。首先从形式上看，英语、汉语都用派生（derivative）和复合（compound）的方式构词。例如：

A（派生）：英语：boyish/childish, foolish, old-maidish…
　　　　　　汉语：孩子气、书生气、傻气、妖气、晦气……
　　　　　　（英语-ish 构成形容词，表示"……似的、有……特征的"。汉语的"……气"也是如此。）

B（复合）：英语：earthquake, housework, playground, footprint, manuscript, mainstream, broadcast

汉语：地震、家务、操场、脚印、手稿、主流、广播

虽然复合词在英语中不断增加，但派生词（A）仍然占主流。汉语则相反，复合形式是词语的主体。从构成形式上看，汉语的复合词包括以下类型：

(1) 并列式

前后成分意思相同或接近：

学习、运动、旅行、洗澡、爱好、道路、人民……

前后成分意思相反或相对：

上下、左右、手足、来往、阴阳、好歹、多少……

(2) 偏正式

前面的成分修饰、限制后面的成分：

车票、现金、高级、电话、黑板、好看……

(3) 主谓式

后面的成分陈述、说明前面的成分：

头疼、目击、性急、年轻、地震、海啸……

(4) 动宾式

前面的是行为，后面的是对象：

有名、吃香、得意、当心、动身、教书、知己……

(5) 补充式

前面是行为，后面说明结果：

改善、提高、推广、说明、破坏、接近、介入、支出……

(6) 重叠式

爸爸、妈妈、哥哥、弟弟、姐姐、妹妹……

汉语复合词、短语（phrase or word-combination）、句子（sentence）的构造方式相同，而英语的词语和句子分别受词法、句法的制约，这是英、汉词语构形差异的主要原因。

除了以上差别外，英语、汉语的词语在功能表现形式上也有不同。比如，英语名词有"数"的不同，动词有人称、时态等变化，动词、形容词转变成名词时一般要有形式上的变化。汉语的名词、动词、形容词没有这些变化。例如：

⑪ I do exercise everyday//Doing exercise is good to your health//I did a lot of exercise last year

我每天锻炼　　　　　锻炼对身体有好处　　　　　我去年经常锻炼

但是，汉语的名词、动词、形容词都有重叠形式，例如：
名 词 重 叠：人人、家家、处处、天天、年年、时时
　　　　　　上上下下、里里外外、前前后后、高高低低、时时刻刻
动 词 重 叠：说说笑笑、来来往往、拉拉扯扯、打打骂骂、磕磕碰碰
　　　　　　考虑考虑、学习学习、锻炼锻炼、休息休息、打扫打扫
　　　　　　吃吃饭、洗洗澡、看看书、睡睡觉、跑跑步
形容词重叠：花花绿绿、洋洋洒洒、干干净净、整整齐齐、漂漂亮亮
　　　　　　红彤彤、绿油油、金灿灿、亮闪闪、暖洋洋/暖融融、凉飕飕

汉语名词、动词、形容词的重叠表达特定的意义，有的还发生作用上的变化。

再从意义上看，英、汉词语有对等，也有不对等的。对等的情况比较简单，比如一些基本物质、自然现象、身体器官、科学研究、工程技术、人文—社会现象等方面的词语，英语和汉语是可以一一对应的，例如：

⑫ water 水　　rain 雨　　mountain 山　　hand 手　　philosophy 哲学
　　gene 基因　　movie 电影　　love 爱情　　law 法律　　divorce 离婚

有些英、汉词语的字面意思、联想意义都可以对应，例如：
⑬ He is as sly as a fox　He is foxy　他滑得像一只狐狸　他是个老狐狸
⑭ You ass!　　　　你这头蠢驴！
⑮ He just parrots what others say　他不过是鹦鹉学舌罢了

英、汉词语意义不对等的情况比较复杂。这里只能简单举例说明：
(a) 英、汉词语不同，但实际上指的是同一事物。例如：
⑯ black tea 红茶　　　　green-eyed 红眼病
　　brown sugar 红糖　　　blue films 黄色电影
　　brown bread 黑面包　　be bruised black and blue 被打得青一块紫一块

(b) 英、汉词语字面上相当，实际上指的不是同一事物。例如：
⑰ rest room（洗手间）≠ 休息室（drawing room/lobby）
　　political campaign（竞选活动）≠ 政治运动（political movements）
　　National Trust（英国文物托管委员会）≠ 国家托拉斯（state trust）

(c) 英语、汉语词语的对应不均衡，汉语要加上其他词语才能与英语对应。比如：
⑱ I borrowed some money from him 我跟他借了些钱
⑲ I lent some money to him 我借给他一些钱

⑳ He took me to the airport 他（用车）带我去机场
㉑ He brought me a gift 他给我带来一个礼物

（d）英、汉词语的感情色彩或表达程度不对等。例如：英语 materialist 表示"讲究实际/物质利益的人"，并不含多少贬义，但是汉语的"物质主义者""物质利益至上的人"却含有贬义。再如：individualism——个人主义（贬义）、ambitious——有抱负的、雄心勃勃的（褒义）、有野心的、野心勃勃的（贬义）。再比如，由于表达习惯的不同，英语的 quite ＋形容词（表示积极含义），一般不如汉语的"相当＋形容词（表示积极含义）"那么肯定和积极。例如：

㉒ She is quite pretty，（but unhealthy-looking.）→ 她有几分姿色，（但看起来不太健康。）

㉓ 她相当漂亮，追她的人相当多。→ She is pretty, and has many pursuers.

3. 英汉表达习惯的比较

最后谈谈英、汉语言表达习惯上的一些异同。这里也只能简单地概括几条：

（a）英、汉语言都讲究表达的得体，对不同语体（style）的遣词造句、表达风格都有明确的区分。例如（转引自邓炎昌、刘润清《语言与文化：英汉语言与文化对比》，外语教学与研究出版社 1989，p. 224）：

㉔
```
      Dr. and Mrs. John Q. Smith           约翰·Q. 史密斯博士及夫人
   Request the pleasure of the company of            敬请
        Mr. And Mrs. Wang Xiaoyan                 王晓燕伉俪
               At a reception
    in honor of the arrival of the ── delegation   莅临欢迎某代表团招待会
           4：30 p.m.，October 6             10月6日下午4时30分
         Pacific Room，Continental Hotel          大陆饭店，太平洋厅
                 R. S. V. P.                        敬请赐复
```

这是同一份请柬的英、汉两种版本，两种语言在称谓、措辞和格式上有共同的特点：文雅、简洁、正式、明确。

（b）英语和汉语的某些习惯表达也体现出共同的思维方式和表达形式，例如：

㉕ strike while the iron is hot 趁热打铁
㉖ many hands make light work 人多好办事
㉗ haste makes waste 欲速则不达
㉘ to let the facts speak for themselves 让事实说话

有些英、汉语言的固定表达看似不同，实际上意思接近，表达方法也相去不远，例如：

㉙ look before you leap 三思而后行

㉚ where there is smoke there is a fire 无风不起浪

㉛ where there is a will there is a way 有志者事竟成

㉜ give a person a dose of his own medicine 以其人之道，还治其人之身

㉝ don't teach your grandma how to suck the egg 别班门弄斧

但是要注意的是，有些看似相同的表达，意思上却有很大差距，例如：英语的 gilding the lily 看似汉语的"锦上添花"，实际上表达的是"画蛇添足"，英语 a miss is as good as a mile 很像汉语的"差之毫厘，失之千里"，实际上指"差一毫米与差一公里同样是差"（错就是错）。英语里有 shut the stable door after the horse has bolted (has been stolen)，指的是"于事无补"，而不是"亡羊补牢"；英语的 to blow one's own horn (or trumpet)，意思是"自吹自擂"，而不是"各吹各的调"（各人做各人的事情）。

(c) 还有一个值得注意的地方，就是英、汉语言对于俗语、套话的态度存在一定差异。英语里有一个法语借词叫"Cliché"（陈词滥调），指反复使用、缺乏新意的成语、俗话（overused idioms），如 a blessing in disguise（塞翁失马）、hit the nail on the head（击中要害）等，也包括 (b) 里面引用过的一些。

汉语对待成语、俗话的态度一般说来要积极得多。汉语中有大量的成语、惯用语、俗语，它们凝聚着千百年来中国人民的智慧和经验；很多成语包含着历史故事，发人深省，给人启迪。这些成语、俗语和惯用语语言精练、含义丰富，在表达上有非常重要的作用。

最后值得一提的是，汉语的一些词语在意义的表达上有一些特殊的方法，例如：

同义修饰——姗姗来迟（be late）、循循善诱（be good at teaching）、肃然起敬（be filled with deep esteem）。

同义相加——全心全意（wholehearted）、坚持不懈（unremitting）、寡廉鲜耻（shameless）、忘恩负义（ungrateful）。

汉语为什么用一个意义相近、相同的词语来修饰另一个词语呢？这个问题值得思考。从表达效果上看，这种同义修饰、同义相加能够起到使意义丰满、表达生动的作用。这种方法也影响到一般的表达，例如：

毫无根据的捏造/谎言 lies/fabrication："捏造/谎言"本来就是毫无根据的

不切实际的幻想 illusions：不切实际正是"幻想"的特点
无私的奉献 dedication：无私是"奉献"的特点
残酷的迫害 persecution："迫害"通常是残酷的
冗长空洞的说教 preach："说教"的特点是空洞、冗长

英汉翻译方法简介
A Brief Introduction to English-Chinese Translation Methods

从上面的比较可以看出，英、汉语言在词语、句子、表达习惯等方面存在着很大差异；英—汉翻译不是把英语的词语、句子翻译成汉语的词语、句子那么简单。学习英—汉翻译，除了要对两种语言有一定的了解外，还应该学习和掌握一些基本的翻译方法。

翻译是把一种语言符号转换成另一种语言符号的语言"中介"活动，真实、准确是翻译的灵魂。真实、准确的含义首先是尊重原文、忠实于原文。同时，翻译又是架设在两种语言、两种文化之间的桥梁，翻译的目的是进行沟通、达成理解。所以，为了既准确体现原文的意思，又使译文符合表达习惯、易于理解，有时需要对译文的结构、词语、表达等进行调整。这是真实、准确的另一层含义。

为了达到真实、准确的翻译效果，英—汉翻译中常采用如下一些方法。

1. 复译（repetition）

为了使译文的表达更加明确，原文里代词所指代的词语、被省略的词语，需要翻译出来。例如：

① Ignorance is the mother of fear as well as of admiration.
   无知是恐惧的根源，也是崇拜的根源。
② Salvation by faith rather than works.
   与其靠善行，不如靠信仰来拯救。
③ He arrived in Johnnesburg from the Transkei, where he was raised to be a chief of the Thembu.
   他从特兰斯凯到了约翰内斯堡，在特兰斯凯，他是被当作坦普族未来的首领来培养的。
④ Reading makes a full man; conference a ready man; and writing an exact man.

读书使人充实，讨论使人机敏，写作使人准确。

2. 增译（amplification）

为了既准确表达原文的意思，又使译文符合表达习惯，易于理解，翻译时需要增加一些词语。例如：

⑤ What a surprise!

多么令人吃惊的事！

⑥ Jack married Lily.

杰克跟莉莉结婚了。

⑦ He has neither phoned nor written us.

他既没有给我们打电话，也没有给我们写信。

⑧ John had some bread and coffee.

约翰吃了点儿面包，喝了点儿咖啡。

⑨ The daughter grew up without a father's guidance.

女儿在没有父亲的指导和庇护下长大。

⑩ Although they are poor, they are happy.

虽然他们很穷，但是很快乐。

3. 省译（omission）

与"增译"相反，对原文中的某些词语省而不译。例如：

⑪ Let the facts speak for themselves.

让事实说话。

⑫ They ran the heater in their car until it ran out of gas.

他们启动汽车里的暖气，直到汽油用光。

⑬ He changed his mind at last minute.

他最后一分钟改变了主意。

⑭ He has made rapid progress this term.

这学期他进步很快。

⑮ try and find it

试着找找

⑯ come and see

来看看

⑰ go and play basketball

去打篮球

4. 转译 (conversion)

为了准确体现原文的意思，译文采用不同性质的词语和结构。例如：

⑱ Fight the fire
  救火

⑲ to be refreshed
  恢复疲劳

⑳ fly economy class
  坐经济舱

㉑ He had an accident at work.
  他在工作中出了事故。

㉒ Something has gone wrong with the engine.
  这台发动机出了毛病。

㉓ Such a goal was impossible of achievement.
  这样的目标是不可能实现的。

㉔ He left without a word.
  他没留下一句话就走了。

㉕ He was involved in working out a plan.
  他专心致志地制订计划。

㉖ He told me that the road was closed.
  他告诉我那条路封闭了。

㉗ He has warned that more oil would be needed that year.
  他警告说当年将需要更多的石油。

㉘ It is well known that the earth is round.
  大家都知道地球是圆的。

㉙ The novel was completed by his wife.
  小说最后是由他的妻子完成的。

5. 倒译 (inversion)

翻译时对词语或语素出现的先后顺序进行调整。例如：

㉚ Northwest
  西北

㉛ Trafalgar Square, London
  伦敦特拉法尔加广场

㉜ back and forth

前前后后地

㉝ upstairs

楼上

㉞ downstairs

楼下

㉟ doubtless

无疑的

㊱ turn left

（向）左转

㊲ on the left of the road

马路的左边

㊳ I came for you.

我为你而来。

㊴ I shall go there tomorrow unless I'm too busy.

如果我不太忙，明天会去那儿。

㊵ It's three days since he left.

他已经走了（离开）三天了。

6. 分译（division）

有时对于比较长的句子，译文需要采用断句并分别翻译的方法；一些意义比较宽泛的词语，有时也需要用不同的词语对它进行分译。例如：

㊶ The boy is quite clever and polite at that.

这孩子很聪明，而且还有礼貌。

㊷ He insisted on buying another house, which he had no use for.

他非要再买一处房子，实际上他完全不需要。

㊸ There was something original, independent, and heroic about the plan that pleased all of them.

那个方案有创意，别出心裁，也很大气，所以人人都喜欢。

㊹ How can you expect your children to be truthful when you yourself tell lies?

你自己讲假话，怎么能期待你的孩子说真话呢？

7. 反译（negation）

不同的语言，肯定、否定的概念和表达方式不完全相同。有时译文需要用相反的表达形式（原文“否定”→译文“肯定”/原文“肯定”→译文“否定”），才能更准确地反映原文的意思、更容易明白。

英语“否定”→译文“肯定”。例如：

㊺ It couldn't be better!

好极了！

㊻ He didn't come until yesterday.

他直到昨天才来。

㊼ They never meet without quarreling.

他们一见面就要吵架。

㊽ These shoes are comfortable rather than pretty.

这双鞋不好看，但是舒服。

㊾ I don't think that's going to happen.

我认为那样的事情不会发生。

英语“肯定”→译文“否定”。例如：

㊿ Students are still arriving.

学生们还没到齐呢。

(51) The team is yet to win a game.

那支球队还未赢过一场比赛。

(52) The teacher really has an open mind.

老师真的没有偏见。

(53) The boat sank off the coast.

船在离海岸不远处沉没了。

(54) This is the last thing I would like to do.

我最不愿意做这种事。

标点符号用法示例
Examples about Punctuation Marks

英语	汉语	用 例
. period	。 句号	Where underground water comes to the surface, there are oases. 哪里有地下水流出地表，哪里就有绿洲。
? question mark	? 问号	We often get in our own way, don't we? 我们常常是自己困扰自己，不是吗？
! exclamation mark	! 叹号	What a fool! 真愚蠢！
, comma	, 逗号	Given the opportunity, she might well have become an outstanding artist. 要是给她机会，她很可能成为一位杰出的艺术家。
, as above	、 顿号	To avoid criticism, do nothing, say nothing, be nothing. 要不想受到批评，你就得什么也不说、什么也不做、什么也不是。
; semicolon	; 分号	The more we do, the more we can do; the busier we are, the more leisure. 做得越多，我们就越能干；时间抓得越紧，就越有空闲。
: colon	: 冒号	What is man's first duty? The answer is brief: to be himself. 人的首要职责是什么？答案很简单：不伪饰自己。
" " quotation marks	" " 引号	The boy asked: "How much is a cream cone?" 男孩问："一个冰淇淋蛋筒多少钱？"

续表

英语	汉语	用 例
( ) parentheses	( ) 括号	You write with ease... But easy writing's curst hard reading. (Richard Brinsley Sheridan) 你轻轻松松地写……但是轻松地写是困难地读的祸根。(理查·布林斯利·谢里登)
— em dash	—— 破折号	That was selective listening—we hear what we want to hear. 这就是有选择地听——听到的都是我们想听的。
... ellipsis	…… 省略号	"When I become a big boy..." This is what a little boy likes to say to himself. "等我长大以后……"小男孩总是喜欢这么对自己说。
	． 着重号	别问他，他什么也不知道。
— en dash	— 连接号	Human beings use only 10－12% of their potential. 人类只使用了自己潜能的10％—12％。
	· 间隔号	Nelson Mandela is the first black president of South Africa. 纳尔逊·曼德拉是南非首位黑人总统。
	《 》 书名号	*The Blue Bistro* is written by Elin Hilderbrand. 《蓝色小酒馆》是艾琳·西德布朗德写的。
	____ 专名号	He lives in Washington D.C.. 他住在华盛顿特区
/ virgule	/ 分隔号	If you ask a person whether s/he thinks him/herself as pretty... 要是你问一个人他或她是否觉得自己漂亮……

21

第一单元　说明文

Unit 1　Exposition

学习目标 Learning Goals

主题 Topics	1. 为什么学外语? 　 Reasons for Studying a Foreign Language 2. 中国古代科技及其影响 　 Science and China's Influence on the World 3. 女性成功的秘密 　 Ten Power Tips: What Are the Real Secrets of Success 4. 运动快餐计划 　 An "Exercise Snack" Plan
翻译技能 Skills	◎ 语序 1：英—汉句子的基本结构；名词、动词 　 译法：分译(division) ◎ 语序 2：比较句；名词、形容词 　 译法：倒译(inversion) ◎ 语序 3：形式主语 　 派生词 　 译法：增译(amplification) ◎ 语序 4："把"字句 　 复合词(1) 　 译法：转译(conversion)

第一课　为什么学外语

Reasons for Studying a Foreign Language

☐ 最近的一项调查发现，学习外语的益处很多。这篇课文以摘要的形式介绍了调查的结果；文章简明扼要，内容通俗而不乏学术性。

☐ 本课的学习重点是了解英、汉句子基本结构的异同和分译的方法。

A new research has identified more than 700 reasons to study languages. It concludes that the strongest of these reasons are the personal benefits and enjoyment that people gain from learning a language. The 700 reasons for studying languages have been grouped into 70 different key areas in which languages make a difference, each area identified by a keyword. The following is the pick of the bunch:

- Academic skill: Language learning develops your skills (i.e. essay writing, research, planning.)
- Accessibility: Everyone can gain benefits from learning a language-cultural enrichment, and the ability to communicate and interact confidently with people outside one's own community.
- Careers: A language broadens your choice of career.
- Communication: Language learning helps to develop communication skills which are really vital if you're applying for a job or just in daily life, you need to be able to communicate.
- Creativity: Plurilinguals as a group think in more flexible and divergent ways than monolinguals as a group: they innovate more, create more new knowledge and dreams.
- Culture: Learning a language does broaden your

Notes:
1. identify:证实、确定
2. area:领域
3. accessibility:沟通能力、亲和力
4. broaden:拓宽、加宽
5. plurilingual:多元语言
6. otherwise:否则、别的
7. protect...from: 使……不受
8. age:衰老、老化
9. intercultural:跨文化的
10. by definition:准确地说

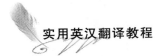

awareness of different cultures—you learn things that you would otherwise never come across.
- Health: Learning and using a second language helps to protect the brain from the effects of ageing.
- Intercultural Competence: Language learning, by definition, is an intercultural experience.
- Learning strategies: Language learning actually helps to develop your memory.
- Values: Language learning promotes tolerance and understanding.

(From Angela Gallagher-Brett, *700 Reasons for Studying Languages*, www.llas.ac.uk / 700 reasons)

1. 根据文章内容回答问题

（1）这是一个什么样的调查？

（2）这项调查的结论是什么？

（3）根据课文内容概括学习外语的用处（如：有助于增加就业机会）。

2. 词语翻译练习

英语里有些词语兼有名词、动词用法，如 research、study、work、drink、cook 等等。这些词语的汉语对应词有的也是名词、动词同形，如 research(v.)研究(动词)/research(n.)研究(名词)、work(v.)工作(动词)/work(n.)工作(名词)。但是也有不是这样对应的，如 group(v.)分组、分类、成群(动词)/group(n.)组、群、团体(名词)。翻译下面的词语，看看它们的对应情况。

experience(n.)_____　　experience(v.)_____
benefit(n.)_____　　benefit(v.)_____

plan(n.) _____   plan(v.) _____
age(n.) _____   age(v.) _____
invention _____   invent _____
enjoyment _____   enjoy _____
creativity _____   create _____
strength _____   strengthen _____

3. 翻译方法

（1）**分译**(division)——把一个比较长的句子翻译成几个较短的句子。结构比较复杂的句子，可以采用分译的方法。例如：

① A new research has identified more than 700 reasons to study languages.
一项新的研究发现，学习外语的原因多达700多种。

② How can you expect your children to be truthful when you yourself tell lies?
你自己讲假话，怎么能期待你的孩子说真话呢？

③ There was something original, independent, and heroic about the plan that pleased all of them.
那个方案有创意，别出心裁，也很大气，人人都喜欢。

（2）分译练习

① It concludes that the strongest of these reasons are the personal benefits and enjoyment that people gain from learning a language.
→

② The 700 reasons for studying languages have been grouped into 70 different key areas in which languages make a difference.
→

③ You learn things that you would otherwise never come across.
→

④ He insisted on buying another house, which he had no use for.
→

4. 语法练习

(1) 英语、汉语的句子结构（"RBD"与"LBD"）

句子一般由主语（subject）、谓语（predicate）和宾语（object）构成。例如：

> He (S)　　borrowed (P)　　a book (O).
> →他(S)　　借了(P)　　一本书(O).

这个句子说明"谁—做了—什么"，英、汉句子的结构、语序相同。但是，除了说明"谁做了什么"，句子经常还要说明"怎么做（How）""为什么做（Why）"等情况。例如：

① He borrowed a book.
② He borrowed a book from the library.
③ He borrowed a book from the library yesterday.
④ He borrowed some books from the library yesterday in order to write the paper.
→

　　　　　　　　　　　　　　　　　　　　　　　他借了一本书。
　　　　　　　　　　　　　　　　　　　　　他从图书馆借了一本书。
　　　　　　　　　　　　　　　　　　他昨天从图书馆借了一本书。
　　　　　　　　　　　　　为了写这篇论文，他昨天从图书馆借了一些书。

上面的例子说明，当增加新的信息时，英语的句子结构向右发展（Right Branching Direction，RBD），而汉语的句子结构向左发展（Left Branching Direction，LBD）。

(2) 练习：把下面的句子译成汉语（注意画线部分的位置，句子太长可以分译）

① Everyone can gain benefits <u>from learning a language</u>.
→

② Learning a language does broaden your awareness <u>of different cultures</u>.
→

③ Plurilinguals as a group think <u>in more flexible and divergent ways than monolinguals as a group</u>.
→

5. 指出并改正译句中的错误

① A language broadens your choice of career.
→外语扩大你的选择职业。

② each area identified by a keyword
→每个领域被代表一个关键词

③ interact confidently with people outside one's own community
→自信地跟人们互动你自己以外的社区

④ develop communication skills which are really vital if you're applying for a job
→发展交流的能力很重要,如果你正要申请一个工作

6. 把下面的儿歌翻译成汉语

例如:That is the malt
　　　that lay in the house that Jack built
　　　——这就是那块放在杰克盖的房子里的麦芽糖。

This is the rat
that ate the malt
that lay in the house that Jack built
→

补充材料(Supplementary Materials)

Arbitrariness in Language

The overwhelming presence of Arbitrariness in language is the chief reason it takes so long to learn the vocabulary of a foreign language: It's generally impossible to guess the meaning of an  unfamiliar word, and each new word just has to be learned individually. This arbitrariness is the reason that the "universal translator" beloved of science-fiction movies is simply impossible. You know the scene: our intrepid space adventurers arrive on a new planet and find an alien race speaking a totally unfamiliar language, so they whip out their machine and twiddle a couple of dials, and—hey presto!—the alien speech is at once rendered into perfect American English. On a more realistic scale, even if you learn a couple of thousand Basque words, if someone says to you "watch out—you might run into a lupu out there", where lupu is a word you don't know, you have no way of knowing whether a lupu might be a bear trap, a poisonous snake, an armed robber or a starving wolf. In fact, it's a scorpion. So much for the universal translator.

(From R. L. Trask, *Language: The Basils*, Routledge, 1995)

Notes:
overwhelming:绝对的、决定性的　　　　arbitrariness:任意性
alien race:异类、外星人　　　　　　　　whip out:迅速拿出
universal translator:万能翻译机、通用翻译器

问题：

① 学习外语词汇为什么要花那么长时间？

② 你觉得"万能翻译机"行得通吗？

翻译：

① dial _____   ② individually _____

③ speech _____   ④ poisonous _____

⑤ realistic _____   ⑥ presence _____

⑦ It's generally impossible to guess the meaning of an unfamiliar word.

⑧ You have no way of knowing whether a lupu might be a bear trap, a poisonous snake, an armed robber or a starving wolf.

Word Meaning and Translation

The variation between languages in the different components and relations of meaning has two consequences for translation. Firstly the meaning that is translated will be decided by situation and context, not by the dictionary; and secondly, the transfer will nearly always involve some form of loss or change.

As Catford says, "The SL (source language) and TL (target language) items rarely have the same 'meaning'." The second consequence of meaning differences between languages is that one task of a linguistic theory of translation becomes that of defining the catalogue of translation techniques required to overcome mismatches.

Concretization. The hyponymic/hypernymic shifts in translation are Concretization or Differentiation, with its corollary Generalization. The German *Geschwister*, for example, could be translated as the more concrete and differentiated *brothers and sisters* or as the more abstract and undifferentiated *siblings*, depending on context and desired effect.

Logical derivation. The English expression *shorter working hours* express the result of an action, whereas the German and French equivalents—*Senkung der Aebeitszeit* and *reduction de la semaine de travail*—express the cause.

Antonymic translation is translation by the opposite, which is frequently used to achieve what is felt to be more natural wording in the target language. Thus the French *est une valeur déjà ancienne* may be translated literally (*is an already old value*) but could also be translated as *is by no means a new value*.

Compensation is a technique used when something in the source language is not translatable. In the film *Man Bites Dog*, a serial killer is having dinner with his friends. In a sudden fit of rage he shoots one of them dead, whereupon a woman who had been using the familiar **tu** prudently switches to the more respectful **vous**. The subtitler compensated for the absence of an equivalent by using the word Sir, a frequent but not always plausible solution.

(From Peter Fawcett, *Translation and Language*, Foreign Language Teaching and Research Press[外研社], 2007)

Notes:
transfer：转换、迁移　　　　　　hyponymic/hypernymic：下位关系/上位关系
equivalent：对应词　　　　　　　logical derivation：逻辑推导、由逻辑推导而来
serial killer：连环杀手

问题：

① 根据短文,什么是"上下位关系"的改变?

② 你能把 concretization、logical derivation、antonymic translation、compensation 这几个词译成中文吗?

③ 请你举出用上面几种方法翻译的例子:
___
___
___
___

第二课　中国古代科技及其影响

Science and China's Influence on the World

□ 本课的材料选自李约瑟（Joseph Needham）的 *The Grand Titration*: *Science and Society in East and West*，简要介绍了 14 世纪中国的科技发明对西方的影响。

□ Dr. Joseph Needham（1900—1995）：李约瑟，英国科学家、皇家学会会员（FRS），著有《中国科学技术史》等，是第一位向世界全面介绍中国古代科技成就的西方人。

□ 本课的学习重点是比较句和倒译。

Notes：
1. Christian era：公元，基督纪元
2. Renaissance：文艺复兴（14—16 世纪）。欧洲古典艺术、建筑、文学等人文主义复兴，起源于 14 世纪的意大利，后来蔓延到整个欧洲，标志着从中世纪到现代时期的过渡。
3. driving-belt：传动带
4. chain-drive：链条传动装置

During the first fourteen centuries of the Christian era, China transmitted to Europe a veritable abundance of discoveries and inventions which were often received by the West with no clear idea of where they had originated. The technical inventions of course traveled faster and further than the scientific thought. But besides all this there were important influences upon nascent modern science during the Renaissance period, and those continued on throughout the eighteenth century.

In technological influences before and during the Renaissance China occupied a quite dominating position. In the body of this contribution we shall mention among other things the efficient equine harness, the technology of iron and steel, the inventions of gunpowder and paper, the mechanical clock, and basic engineering devices such as the driving-belt, the chain-drive, and the standard method of converting rotary to rectilinear motion, together with segmental arch bridges and nautical techniques such as the stern-post rudder. The world owes far more to the relatively silent craftsmen of ancient and medieval China than to the

中国古代观测天象的仪器

5. stern-post rudder：艉（柱）舵
6. medieval：中世纪的
7. Alexandrian：亚历山大时代的（古希腊）
8. legacy：遗产
9. effect：实现、达到
10. Galilean：伽利略的，基督徒

Alexandrian mechanics, articulate theoreticians though they were.

Thus in relation to the "legacy" of China we have to think of three different values. There is the value of that which helped directly to effect the Galilean break-though, the value of that which became incorporated in modern science later on, and last but not least the value of that which had no traceable influence and yet renders Chinese science and technology no less worthy of study and admiration than that of Europe.

(From Dr. Joseph Needham, *The Grant Titration：Science and Society in East and West*, Routledge, 2005, first published in 1969, Oxford)

1. 根据文章内容回答问题

（1）作者认为14世纪中国对欧洲有过什么影响？

（2）课文所说"中国遗产"的价值在哪些方面？

2. 词语翻译练习

英语有些名词、形容词之间有派生（derivative）关系，汉语的对应词有些是一致的，如 education/educational 教育/教育（的）、health/healthy 健康/健康（的）；有些则不一致，如 confidence/confident 信心/自信（的）、person/personal 人/私人的。请翻译下面的词语，看看它们对应的情况。

awareness _____   aware _____
poison _____   poisonous _____
competence _____   competitive _____
technic _____   technical _____

mechanic _____   mechanical _____
culture _____   cultural _____

3. 翻译方法

（1）**倒译**（inversion）——翻译时对词语或语素出现的先后顺序进行调整。有的书上把词语前后位置的颠倒细分为"倒译"和"移译"（shift）。为了简便起见，这里一概称为"倒译"。例如：

downstairs 楼下　　　　upstairs 楼上
northwest 西北　　　　back and forth 前前后后地
doubtless 无疑的　　　on the left of the road 马路的左边
turn left (向)左转　　Trafalgar Square, London 伦敦特拉法尔加广场
I came for you. 我是为你来的。
It's three days since he left. 他已经走了（离开）三天了。

（2）倒译练习

① the "legacy" of China
→

② the first fourteen centuries of the Christian era
→

③ craftsmen of ancient and medieval China
→

④ where they had originated
→

⑤ articulate theoreticians though they were
→

⑥ The technical inventions of course traveled faster and further than the scientific thought.
→

4. 语法练习

(1) "比"字句

前一课的"语法练习"部分说明,英语句子结构是 RBD,汉语是 LBD。英语、汉语的比较句(comparative patterns)也表现出 RBD 与 LBD 的不同。例如:

① Plurilinguals as a group think in more flexible and divergent ways <u>than monolinguals as a group</u>.

多语人群<u>比单一语言人群</u>的思想更灵活、更多样化。

或:<u>与单一语言的人群相比</u>,多语人群思想更灵活、更多样化。

② The technical inventions of course traveled faster and further <u>than the scientific thought</u>.

技术发明当然<u>比科学思想</u>传播得更快、更远。

或:<u>比起科学思想来</u>,技术发明当然传播得更快、更远。

(2) 把下面的句子译成汉语(注意画线部分的位置,句子太长可以分译)

① The world owes far more to the relatively silent craftsmen of ancient and medieval China <u>than to the Alexandrian mechanics</u>. (owe far more to 更应该感谢,relatively silent 较少记载的,Alexandrian mechanic 亚历山大时代的机械师/技工)

→

② (of that which had no traceable influence and yet) renders Chinese science and technology no less worthy of study and admiration <u>than that of Europe</u> (render 使得)

→

5. 指出并改正译句中的错误

① (and those) continued on throughout the eighteenth century

→(那些影响)持续在整个 18 世纪

②(of that which) helped directly to effect the Galilean break-through
→有助于直接实现了基督徒的突破

③(of that which) became incorporated in modern science later on
→融合到现代科学以后

④(which) were often received by the West with no clear idea of where they had originated
→西方人接受了不知道哪里它们来的

6. 讨 论

(1) 有人认为要学好一门外语,必须学会用这种外语思考,你同意这种看法吗?

(2) 谈谈在你们国家历史上科技发明、思想文化对外交流的情况。

补充材料(Supplementary Materials)

Western Names for China

The best known Western names for China were probably Seres, Sina, and Cathay. Seres comes from the Chinese ssu(丝) silk, and was transmitted to Europe as ser by the Greeks; it had obvious connotations with the silk trade from perhaps as early as 220 B.C.. Sina is Latin and from it we derive our name China, but it seems to have come not from Rome but in the second century B.C. by way of India: it is a corruption of a Sanskrit form of the Chinese dynasty name Chhin.

Later dynasties gave rise to other names, and the tenth-century tribal name of Chhi-tan Liao was transformed to the Russian Khitai; this became the European Cathay referred to the same country, just as there had been in classical times over Sina and the Seres, but in each case the doubt seems to have arisen because one name had arrived overland transmission, the other by sea.

(From Colin A. Ronan, *An Abridgement of Joseph Needham's Original Text*, Cambridge Uniersity Press, 1978)

Notes:

connotation:含义   Chhin:秦(代)

as early as:早在……   Chhi-tan:契丹(辽代)

问题：

① "Sina"这个词是怎么来的？

② 为什么西方语言里"中国"会有这么多称呼？

翻译：

① The best known Western names for China were probably Seres, Sina and Cathay.

② It had obvious connotations with the silk trade from perhaps as early as 220 B.C..

Confucius

By what canon shall we include Confucius and omit Buddha and Christ? By this alone, that he was a moral philosopher rather than a preacher of religious faith; that his call to the noble life was based upon secular motives rather than upon supernatural considerations; that he far more resembles Socrates than Jesus.

Born (552 B.C.) in an age of confusion, in which the old power and glory of China had passed into feudal disintegration and factional strife, Kung-fu-tse undertook to restore health and order to his country. How? Let him speak:

The illustrious ancients, when they wished to make clear and to propagate the highest virtues in the world, put their states in proper order. Before

putting their states in proper order, they regulating their families. Before regulating their families they cultivated their own selves. Before cultivating their own selves they perfected their souls. Before perfecting their souls, they tried to be sincere in their thoughts. Before trying to be sincere in their thought, they extended to the utmost their knowledge. Such investigation of knowledge lay in the investigation of things, and in seeing them as they really were. ...

Here is a sound moral and political philosophy within the compass of a paragraph. ...

A pupil having asked him should one return good for evil, Confucius replied: "With what then will you recompense kindness? Return good for good, and for evil, justice." He did not believe that all men were equal; it seemed to him that intelligence was not a universal gift.

A great city, Chung-tu, took him at his word and made him magistrate. "A marvelous reformation," we are told, "ensued in the manners of the people… There was an end of crime… Dishonesty and dissoluteness hid their heads."… (After his death) His disciples built huts near his grave and remained there, mourning as for a father, for nearly three years. When all of the others were gone, Tse-Kung, who had loved him beyond the rest, continued by the grave for three years more, alone.

(From Will Durant, *Ten Great Thinkers, Adventures in Genius*, Simon and Schuster, New York, 1931)

Notes:
Confucius：孔子，中国古代思想家、教育家，儒家学派创始人。
canon：标准、原则　　　　　　　Buddha：佛、菩萨（释迦牟尼）
Christ：基督　　　　　　　　　　Socrates：苏格拉底（古希腊哲学家）
Jesus：耶稣、耶稣基督　　　　　Kung-fu-tse：孔夫子（i.e.孔子）
return good for evil：以德报怨　　return good for good：以德报德
Tse-Kung：子贡（孔子的学生）

问题：
① 本文作者为什么把孔子列为十大思想家之一？

② 孔子的抱负是什么？

翻译：
① after his death

② There was an end of crime.

③ It seemed to him that intelligence was not a universal gift.

④ A great city, Chung-tu, took him at his word and made him magistrate.

第三课 女性成功的秘密

Ten Power Tips: What Are the Real Secrets of Success?

□ 女性如何获得成功？本文作者给出了十大忠告。这些忠告也许对所有人都有一些启发意义——尽管对"成功"的理解可能见仁见智。

□ 本课的学习重点是形式主语的翻译和增译。

What are the real secrets of success? Here's what some proven winners say:

Be competitive—"To succeed in business you have to want to win," says Liz Lange, founder and president of Liz Lange Maternity. "Too often, women feel they have to be nice. Don't," says Lange.

It's not about friendship—"Women want everyone to like them, but it doesn't really matter what people think of you," says Renee Edelman, senior VP of Edelman. "It's that you get the job done and deliver results."

Stand up for yourself—Restaurateur Donatella Arpaia is responsible for two restaurants and 140 people. "I protect my interests, their interests. If someone is going to mess with that, I cut them out like cancer."

Trust your instincts—Dozens of people tried to talk Lange out of growing her business, now a major force with nationwide distribution at Target. "There are a lot of naysayers out there," says Lange. "Shut out negative noise and go for it."

Always project confidence—Oscar-winning film

Notes:
1. president: 总统、校长、总裁/董事长
2. think of: 想、有……看法、考虑
3. deliver result: 拿出结果
4. restaurateur: 餐馆/饭店老板、业主
5. mess with: 搞砸、惹麻烦
6. naysayer: 反对者、唱反调的人
7. project: 表现出、透出
8. instead: 相反地

producer Cathy Schulman says presentation is key. "When someone asks 'How are you?' don't go into a litany of what's wrong with your life," says Schulman. <u>Instead</u>, present yourself as in control and happy.

Own your success—Say goodbye to fear and insecurity, says Arpaia. Have confidence in your decisions, and make them.

Reach out to other women—When Lange started her business, she called every woman (and man) she admired and asked to meet. "Don't be shy," she says. Schulman begins each day by noting colleagues' accomplishments with a quick call or e-mail. "We don't have golf so create other communities of support."

Insist on being well paid—Don't view wanting money as inelegant or "not classy," says Schulman. "Men make decisions on the bottom line. Why shouldn't we?"

It's OK to make mistakes—When Arpaia realized a business partner-ship was doomed, she cut ties and moved on. "Don't obsess over things," she says.

Be a problem-solver—If something on Schulman's desk seems difficult to deal with, she tackles it first. "Big problems are an opportunity to grow."

(From Julie Scelfo, *Newsweek*, New York: Sept. 25, 2006. Vol. 148)

1. 根据文章内容回答问题

（1）为什么作者说这些秘密是"power tips"？

（2）他们是谁？（Who's who?）
　　　Cathy Schulman
　　　Renee Edelman
　　　Liz Lange
　　　Donatella Arpaia

（3）把课文中的建议翻译出来。

2. 词语翻译练习

翻译下面的词语，注意英—汉词语派生（derivation）方式的异同。

creativity _____   flexibility _____
industrialization _____   concretization _____
broaden _____   strengthen _____
mislead _____   misunderstand _____
possible _____   plausible _____
partnership _____   friendship _____
profit-making _____   Oscar-winning _____

3. 翻译方法

（1）增译（amplification）——为了既准确表达原文的意思，又使译文符合目标语（target language）的表达习惯，易于理解，翻译时需要增加一些词语。例如（增加的部分加上了括号）：

a. 增加名词/名词短语

① Oscar-winning film producer
    获得奥斯卡（奖）的电影制片人

② cultural enrichment
    丰富文化（知识）

③ chain-drive
    用链条传送动力（的装置）

④ The 700 reasons for studying language have been grouped into 70 different key areas.
    （研究人员）把学习语言的700个理由分成70个不同的核心领域。

b. 增加动词/动词短语

⑤ Language learning, be definition, is an intercultural experience.
    学习外语，准确地（说），是一种跨文化的经验。

⑥ I protect my interests, their interests.
    我保护自己的利益，（也保护）他们的利益。

⑦ John had some bread and coffee.
    约翰（吃了）点儿面包，（喝了）点儿咖啡。

⑧ the meaning that is translated will be decided by situation and context, not by the dictionary

要翻译的意思由当时的情景和上下文决定,而不是由词典(决定)

c. 增加量词

⑨ a new research

最新的一(项)研究

⑩ 700 reasons

700(种/个)理由

⑪ a blue and white painted porcelain of Yuan Dynasty

一(件)元代青花瓷器

d. 增加介词/介词短语

⑫ Jack married Lily.

杰克(跟)莉莉结婚了。

⑬ He has neither phoned nor written us.

他既没(给我们)打电话,也没(给我们)写信。

⑭ I cut them out like cancer.

我(把)他们"切除",就像(切除)肿瘤一样。

e. 增加副词、连词

⑮ (but in each case the doubt seems to have arisen) because one name had arrived overland transmission, the other by sea

因为一个名字从陆地传播,(而)另一个从海上(传播)

⑯ Although they are poor, they are happy.

他们虽然(很)穷,(但是很)快乐。

(2) 增译练习

① (Arpaia is responsible for) two restaurants and 140 people

→

② Cathy Schulman says presentation is key.

→

③ present yourself as in control and happy

→

④ We don't have golf so create other communities of support.
→

⑤ to protect brain from the effects of ageing
→

⑥ He was a moral philosopher rather than a preacher of religious faith.
→

⑦ (But besides all this there were important influences upon nascent modern science during the Renaissance period,) and those continued on throughout the eighteenth century.
→

4. 语法练习

（1）句子的主语（subject）

第一课、第二课"语法练习"介绍了英、汉句子结构的不同特点（RBD 和 LBD）。这里再以"主语"的位置为例，说明英、汉句子结构的不同特点。

a. 在英语的 it（形式）主语句里，真正的主语在后面（右边）。在相应的汉语句子里，主语在前面（左边）。例如：

① It doesn't really matter what people think of you, It's that you get the job done and deliver results.
人们怎么看你并不重要；你把事情做好、拿出结果来，这才真的重要。

② It is offensive to make such comparison.
做这种比较是令人不快的。

③ It was far-sighted of her to buy up that property.
她买下那笔财产真是有远见。

b. 表示存在意义的句子里，英语、汉语也表现出 RBD 与 LBD 的不同：

英语——存在（existential there V）＋存在的东西＋地方/时间
汉语——地方/时间＋存在（existential there V）＋存在的东西

例如：

④ There is a dangerous intersection at one end of the block. Before a stop sign was put up, there were ninety accidents there in a year.
街区的尽头有一个危险的路口，在禁行标志竖起之前，一年有 90 起事故。

⑤ There was an end of crime.
犯罪停止了。

（2）把下面的句子译成汉语（把画线部分变成主语）

① It's OK to make mistakes.
　→

② It takes so long to learn the vocabulary of a foreign language.
　→

③ It's generally impossible to guess the meaning of an unfamiliar word.
　→

④ There are a lot of naysayers out there.
　→

⑤ There's no free lunch when it comes to losing weight.
　→

⑥ There was something original about the plan.
　→

5. 指出并改正译句中的错误

① To succeed in business you have to want to win
　→成功在商业你得想赢

② Have confidence in your decisions
→ 有信心对你的决定

③ It takes longer to go there by bus than by bicycle
→ 去那儿还慢坐汽车比骑自行车

④ There was equal preference for part-time work among both men and women
→ 对工作半天有同样的偏爱在男性和女性中间

⑤ Don't obsess over things
→ 别困扰那些事情

6. 讨论

(1) 有些成功的女性被称为"女强人",你怎么看这个词?
(2) 你认为在现代社会里女性成功的有利条件和不利条件有哪些?

补充材料(Supplementary Materials)

Changing Roles of Women in Europe

Recent research into the role of women in society uncovered evidence of considerable cultural diversity even between the industrialized countries of Western Europe. When women aged 18-65 were asked in a cross-national European study, "Which if any of these groups of people lend the greatest support in various ways to women generally in their lives?" it appeared that "their

family" was seen as most supportive, named by between 71% and 80% of those responding: in Britain, 64% also saw "their friends" as lending support, whereas the figures were only 23% for Italy and 17% for Spain.

One striking conclusion to be drawn from this comparison is that in both Britain and Italy there was equal preference for part-time work among both men and women, while in the other countries, notably Germany, the figures were close, not to say identical. Even within Europe, the survey brought out considerable differences in what women hoped to get from their wok. In Britain, flexible working hours were clearly most highly valued, with job security ranking second, while fewer than one in three attached importance to having stimulating or challenging work. In Italy, however, interesting work was a matter of concern to 51%, and in France to 44%. In Spain, job security was thought to be the most import aspect of work. Britain women put high priority on employer provision of childcare.

(From Robert M. Worcester, *World Culture Report* 2000, UNESCO Press)

Notes:
cross-national European study：欧洲跨国研究　　draw a conclusion：得出结论
part-time work：部分时间工作、兼职工作
not to say identical：虽然不完全相同
job security：工作稳定　　　　　　　　　　　one in three：三分之一

问题：① 英国职业女性最看重工作的哪一面？

② 这次调查发现工业化国家女性的什么特点？

翻译：① women aged 18—65

_____

② put high priority on employer provision of childcare

_____

③ it appeared that "their family" was seen as most supportive

Battle of the Sexes: Do Men and Women Lie Differently?

So who's more honest, men or women? It looks like both sexes tend to be equally culpable, though our survey suggests that each is devilish in different ways.

Men's dishonesty surfaces more around impersonal objects. They take office supplies (71% of men vs. 61% women), fudge tax returns (24% vs. 15%) and illegally download music (43% vs. 35%) more often than women.

"Men are more risk-taking," says psychologist Michael Lewis of the Robert Wood Johnson Medical School in New Brunswick, New Jersey. They initiate dishonest acts, while women tend to wait for an opportunity to present itself, and then take advantage. "Women are also doing more lying in the realm of relationships," says Lewis. Although these behaviors are not exclusive to either sex, they are dominant tendencies.

At work, women may not steal supplies as often as men, but they are more likely to lie to the boss about a sick day (64% women vs. 58% men). And in their personal lives, women use dishonesty to avoid conflict, like by fibbing about the cost of a recent purchase (34% women vs. 25% men), or to spare another person's feelings, as in "Those pants don't make your hips look big at all!" (74% vs. 65%).

(From Cynthia Dermody, *Reader's Digest*, Jan. 2004)

Notes:
fudge tax returns:用伪造的方法骗得退税　　illegally:非法(地)
wait for an opportunity to present itself:等待机会到来
at work:在工作场所　　fibbing:编无伤大雅的谎话
purchase:购物、购买　　spare another person's feelings:不伤害别人的感情

问题：
① 举例说明男性会在哪一方面不诚实。

② 在个人生活方面女性会撒什么样的谎？

翻译：
① men are more risk-taking

② women may not steal supplies as often as men

③ women tend to wait for an opportunity to present itself, and then take advantage

第四课 运动快餐计划

An "Exercise Snack" Plan

If you are a couch potato, it must be frustrating to keep hearing how good exercise is for your health. It needn't be. Many people have more opportunities to exercise than they realize—a program for health and fitness can be as simple as walking and moving more throughout the day. Here is a plan to help you find the mix of opportunities and activities that will work for you.

- Find the time, with "exercise snacks". The first step is to mine your daily routines to find it. Research shows that you can begin to tap into the health benefits of exercise through many forms of physical activity—using "exercise snacks" that last as little as 10 minutes at a time. Examples? Pacing in your office while you are on the phone, taking the stairs instead of the elevator, trekking up the stairs at home during a TV commercial break. Or break up the day with two-minute walks—for example, to the mailbox, or in a loop around your office corridor.

- Ramp it up. The benefits of these exercise snacks begin to kick in when you burn about 100 calories a day—that's the equivalent of walking a mile. However, many health organizations recommend 30 minutes of moderate activity, which burns about

☐ 制定一项运动计划也许并不那么复杂。课文介绍了日常生活中的一些快餐式运动,健康原来唾手可得。

☐ 课文采用谈话体风格,句式富于变化,学习重点是"把"字句和转译。

Notes:

1. couch potato:终日懒散的人(整天坐着或躺着看电视)
2. work for you:对你很合适、有用、有效
3. tap into:接近、发掘
4. ramp it up:(此处比喻)设定更高目标
5. kick in:(好处)的实现、兑现
6. resistance training:耐力训练
7. provided (conj.):假如、要是
8. level ground:平地
9. only to:结果却……、不料竟……
10. fall off the wagon:半途而废
11. on the right track:想得对、做得对

12. USDA: 美国农业部
(United States Department of Agriculture)

210 calories, on most days of the week. A long-term study of Harvard alumni showed the lowest death rates in those who burned at least 300 calories a day in exercise or activity.

- That's not very hard to do. You may hate to sweat, dislike the gym or lack the time or resolve to fit sessions of <u>resistance training</u> or stretching into your busy week. But you can accomplish the same thing through gardening, house cleaning, ballroom or square dancing, hiking, cycling and other activities. A 165-pound person who spends 30 minutes actively playing with children burns 187 calories, a 200-pound person who cleans out gutters for half an hour burns 227 calories. Walking is often underrated as a form of exercise. Walking slowly burns about five calories per minute, walking briskly burns seven calories per minute and jogging burns roughly nine calories per minute. <u>Provided</u> you're walking on <u>level ground</u>, 80 steps per minute would be considered a slow pace, while moderate to brisk would be 100 steps per minute.

- Keep it up. If you see benefits—and most people do—you're likely to continue with your program. You may not lower your cholesterol or trim your waistline in a few weeks, but you can enjoy the byproducts of physical activity—increased energy, less stress, feeling fitter and sleeping better.

Adapting a new healthy habit, or dropping an unhealthy one, is a process. Many people launch an exercise program <u>only to</u> <u>fall off the wagon</u> a few months later. It's not unusual for this to happen several times before a new habit is firmly established, whether it's quitting smoking or eating less fat. If you're even thinking about incorporating more physical activity into your life, you're <u>on the right track</u>.

The 2005 <u>USDA</u> guidelines state that it may take about 60 minutes of moderate physical activity per day to prevent weight gain, and at least 60 to 90 minutes a day may be needed to maintain weight loss.

While "exercise snacks" can help your health, there's no free lunch when it comes to losing weight.

(From Howard Hartley, M.D., I-Min Lee, SC.D. Nancy Ferrari, *Newsweek*, New York: Mar. 26, 2007. Vol. 149)

1. 根据文章内容回答问题

1. 举例说明什么是"运动快餐"。

2. 对哈佛大学校友的长期研究有什么结果?

3. 体育运动的"副产品"(附带的好处)有什么?

2. 词语翻译练习

英语中的复合词(compounds),有些可以用汉语的复合词对译,如,eyesight 视力、guideline 方针/指南、safeguard 维护/保护;有的则要用短语(phrase)来翻译,如,lifesaving 挽救生命的、yourself 你自己。请翻译下面的词语,并说说汉语哪些是词、哪些是短语。

keyword _____   interact _____
otherwise _____   overcome _____
nationwide _____   download _____
mailbox _____   underrate _____
waistline _____   ballroom _____
byproduct _____

3. 翻译方法

(1) 转译(conversion)——为了准确体现原文的意思,译文采用不同性质的词语和结构。常见的有词性的转换和结构的转换。例如:

a. 词性的转换

① eat less fat

少吃肥肉(less: adj. → 少: adv.)

② but you can enjoy the byproducts of physical activity
但是你可以享受运动带来的副产品（of：prep.→带来的：v.+的）

③ —while you're on the phone
——你接电话的时候（be on the phone→接电话：vp.）

④ despite the lifesaving potential of the technology
尽管这项技术具有挽救生命的潜力（the...potential of...：np.→具有……的潜力：vp.）

b. 结构的转换

⑤ insist on being well paid
坚持要求较高的薪水（被动→主动）

⑥ the alien speech is at once rendered into perfect American English
外星人的话立刻变成了标准的美国英语（被动→主动）

c. 词和短语之间的转换

⑦ women use dishonesty to avoid conflict
女人撒谎为的是避免冲突（to→为的是）

⑧ (which became incorporated in modern science) later on
后来（变成近代科学的组成部分）（later on→后来）

(2) 转译练习

① Women feel they have to be nice
→

② In spite of the weather, they decided to go
→

③ Arpaia is responsible for two restaurants
→

④ There are a lot of naysayers out there
→

⑤ —that's the equivalent of walking a mile
→

⑥ —increased energy, less stress...
→

⑦ at least 60 to 90 minutes a day may be needed to maintain weight loss
→

4. 语法练习

(1) "把"字句

"把"字句也是一种向左发展的结构(LBD)。例如,lower your cholesterol(降低你的胆固醇)、trim your waistline(缩小你的腰围)都是 V(verb)→O(object)的自然顺序(RBD),"把"字句是把"V(verb)→O(object)"变成"O(object)←V(verb)"。

V(verb)→O(object)	动词→宾语		"把"	O(object)←V(verb)	
lower your cholesterol	降低	你的胆固醇	把	你的胆固醇	降低
trim your waistline	缩小	你的腰围	把	你的腰围	缩小

再如:

① drop an unhealthy one

　　丢掉一个不健康的习惯/把一个不健康的习惯丢掉

② (a 200-pound person who cleans out gutters for half an hour) burns 227 calories

　　消耗(燃烧)227卡路里/把227卡路里消耗掉(燃烧掉)

在LBD结构里,新的、重要的信息放在左边(left);所以"把"字句里的宾语(O)是一个重要的信息。当我们谈论锻炼身体时,"胆固醇""腰围""卡路里"当然是重要的话题;使胆固醇、腰围或者卡路里发生变化(降低、缩小或消耗掉),可能就是我们运动的目的。下面的(b)就表现了这种目的:

③ I burned 360 calories.

(a) 我消耗了360卡路里。　　　(b) 我把360卡路里消耗掉了。

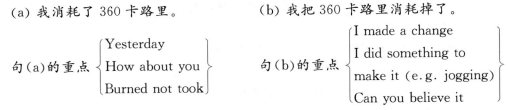

(2) 用"把"字句翻译下面的句子

① (30 minutes of moderate activity can) burn about 210 calories.

→

② In Britain 64% saw "their friends" as leading support.

→

③ (if someone is going to mess with that) I cut them out like cancer.
　→

④ Don't view wanting money as inelegant or "not classy".
　→

⑤ (if something on her desk seems difficult to deal with) she tackles it first.
　→

⑥ to fit sessions of resistance training into your busy week.
　→

5. 指出并改正译句中的错误

① I forgot my key in the car
　→我忘了钥匙在车里

② (in a sudden fit of rage) he shoots one of them dead
　→他开枪杀他们中的一个死了

③ (before) a new habit is established
　→一个新的习惯被形成

④ you're on the right track
　→你在对的道路上

⑤ he had an accident at work
　→他在工作中有了事故

⑥ Each new word has to be learned individually.
→每个新词都要一个一个地被学会。

6. 讨论

（1）你听过下面这些说法吗？能不能把它们翻译成英语？

　　饭后百步走，活到九十九。

　　生命在于运动。

（2）用课文里的方法，算算你一天大概消耗多少卡路里。

补充材料（Supplementary Materials）

Tea Boosts Immunity and Helps Skin

Next to water, tea may be the most commonly consumed drink on the planet. Now, new researches add to increasing evidence that tea is not only a much-loved beverage, but may offer a host of health benefits as well. A new study reveals how substances found in tea may help prime the body's immune system to fight off infection. Another report shows how substances in green tea may be linked to skin-cell rejuvenation.

This latest study shows how Chemicals—known as alkylamines—which are commonly present in tea (as well as wine, apples, mushrooms, and other sources), are also present in some bacteria, cancerous cells, parasites, fungi, and other disease-causing agents. Drinking tea may be able to prime the body's immune system against these agents, by teaching disease-fighter immune cells to recognize and remember alkylamines, said study co-author Jack F. Bukowski, immunologist at Brigham and Women's Hospital and Harvard Medical School in Boston, Massachusetts. Bukowski's team carried out experiments which revealed that exposing blood to these chemicals in the test tube could increase the size of one type of defensive response to simulated infection by up to five times. In contrast, human blood cells not exposed to alkylamines showed a much less significant response to simulated bacterial infection.

Stephen Hsu, an expert on tea-related health issues and cell biologist at the Medical College of Georgia, Augusta, has published his own study in the *Journal of Pharmacology and Experimental Therapeutics*, revealing that other chemicals found in tea are able to reactivate dying skin cells. The finding could one day possibly be applied not only to anti-aging remedies but also to wound healing and the treatment of skin conditions, said Hsu. Some anti-aging cosmetics already contain tea extracts, he said, though their effectiveness has not been scientifically proven.

(From John Pickrell, *National Geography*, Apr. 29, 2003)

Notes:
next to：仅次于
much-loved：深受喜爱的、广受欢迎的
disease-causing agent：引起疾病的物质（媒介）、病因
cell biologist：细胞生物学家
as well：（除了）也/还
chemical：化学成分

问题：
① 喝茶为什么有助于身体对抗疾病？

② 茶叶中的化学成分对于皮肤有什么好处？

翻译：

① exposing blood to these chemicals in the test tube

② increase the size of one type of defensive response to simulated infection by up to five times

③ The finding could one day possibly be applied not only to anti-aging remedies but also to wound healing and the treatment of skin conditions.

New Cancer Scanner Could Be a Sun-lover's Lifesaver

  Skin cancers comprise 81 percent of all new cancers diagnosed in Australia annually. More than 382,000 people are treated for skin cancer each year and more than 1300 die from the disease in that time. Now a simple scanner that can detect skin cancer at an early stage could help save lives and stop thousands of Australians needlessly going under the knife.

  The pioneering SIA scope helps doctors distinguish malignant moles from benign ones by assessing the melanin, collagen and colour of the lesion up to 2mm below the skin's surface. Sydney general practitioner Kerryn Phelps said it was important "not only to prevent but to detect skin cancer as early as possible, and if this means doctors are able to detect skin cancer early then we are talking about life-saving technology".

  Peta Logan, 28, a lifesaver at North Bondi, in Sydney's east, called the procedure a "reality check". After having her moles tested, Ms Logan said although she was "reassured" that her lesions were benign, she was still concerned about the amount of time she had to spend in the sun as part of her lifesaving duties.

"This mole test definitely makes me more aware and I think I should get checked regularly," she said. "I cover up and wear a high-factor sunscreen, but that's not always enough."

Despite the lifesaving potential of the technology, Dr. Phelps, who is one of 70 doctors across Australia to have installed the scanner in their practice, warned it was no substitute for the basic rules of skin cancer prevention.

(From Sarah Taylor, *The Australian*, Feb. 5, 2007)

Notes:
scanner:扫描仪　　　　　　general practitioner:全科医生

问题:
为什么这种扫描仪被称为"救生员"?

翻译:
① More than 382,000 people are treated for skin cancer each year.

② It was important not only to prevent but to detect skin cancer as early as possible.

第二单元 记叙文

Unit 2 Narration

学习目标 Learning Goals

主题 Topics	5. 叱咤风云 The Man of the Moment 6. 要做真正的美国人 The Struggle to Be an All American Girl 7. 冰雪不归路 An Arduous and Determined Trek
翻译技能 Skills	◎ 语序5：被动句 　复合词(2)；"着"的翻译 　译法：省译(omission) ◎ 修饰成分(定语)的翻译 　复合词(3) 　译法：复译(repetition) ◎ 修饰成分(状语)的翻译 　短语的对应(1) 　时间表达；"了"和"过"

第五课 叱咤风云

The Man of the Moment

□ 课文介绍纳尔逊·曼德拉的事迹——他为种族平等与和平解放奋斗的历程，政治上的磨难与家庭生活的创伤。

□ 文章语言平实、夹叙夹议。学习重点是被动句和省译。

Notes:
1. Nelson Mandela：纳尔逊·曼德拉（1918— ）
2. Nobel Peace Prize：诺贝尔和平奖
3. Johnnesburg：约翰内斯堡（南非城市）
4. Young turks：青年激进派
5. African National Congress：非洲人国民大会，简称"非国大"（ANS），南非政党。
6. CIA：中央情报局
7. chauffeur：[法]司机
8. Winnie：温妮（曼德拉前妻）
9. Durban：德班（南非城市）

At political rallies he is treated like a pop star. Young girls scream, young men shout his name and everyone from small children to the elderly push closer to get a glimpse of the man affectionately known by his clan name: "Madiba". Where he ascends the speaker's podium, the roar of the crowd is deafening.

For the last four years, Nelson Mandela has traveled South Africa and the world promoting his vision of racial reconciliation. His tireless campaigning and his undying commitment to the cause of non-racialism have won him a Nobel Peace Prize and made him a global symbol of hope in a post-cold-war era of ethnic strife and instability. But now, with the elections behind him, Mandela must transform the dream that has sustained him into the reality of a new, multiracial South Africa.

Born to lead. He arrived in Johnnesburg from the Transkei. At Fort Hare University, he met the man who would be his life-long compatriot, Oliver Tambo. The two opened the country's first black law practice and together led the Young turks who transformed the African National Congress from an elitist moderate organization to one of mass struggle. When the ANC was banned by the white government in 1960, Mandela went underground and became the first commander of a newly formed guerrilla wing, Spear or the Nation. In 1962, after American CIA agent Millard Shirley tipped off security officials, Mandela was arrested while disguised as a chauffeur outside the town of Howick in Natal.

Mandela often says he has few regrets about his prison years, but his deepest source of sadness is the toll his imprisoning took on his family: His wife Winnie was hounded and harassed for decades, and his daughters grew up without a father's guidance. The marriage came apart after Mrs. Mandela's 1991 conviction for kidnapping and assault and reports of her involvement with a younger man. At 75, Mandela is one of the oldest leaders to be elected president in his country. Though he suffered from tuberculosis in prison, he remains healthy and arises each day at 4:30 to exercise and eat a traditional South African breakfast of cold porridge and fruit. Those closest to him say it is his democratic dream that drives him. "We stand for majority rule, but we don't stand for black majority rule," he reminded the crowd of 150,000 in Durban. "What we stand for is the result of a democratic process."

(选自 Eric Ransdell, Jerelyn Eddings,《爱的教训》,西安交通大学出版社,1997)

1. 根据文章内容回答问题

(1) 曼德拉为什么获得诺贝尔和平奖?

(2) 在曼德拉被监禁的岁月里,他的家庭付出了怎样的代价?

(3) 根据课文内容,说说曼德拉晚年的身体和起居情况。

2. 词语翻译练习

(1) **汉语的复合词**(compounds)

汉语的词语中,复合形式占主流。从构成形式上看,汉语的复合词包括并列式(parataxis)、偏正式(adjunct-head)、主谓式(subject-predicate)、动宾式(verb-object)、补充式(verb-complement)、重叠式(reduplication)。这里先介绍前三种形式。

并列式：
a) 前后两个成分意思相同或接近。例如：
学习、运动、洗澡、爱好、道路、人民
b) 前后两个成分意思相反、相对。例如：
上下、左右、来往、阴阳、好歹、多少

偏正式：
前面的成分修饰限制后面的成分。例如：
高级、电话、黑板、好看、车票、现金

主谓式：
后面的成分陈述说明前面的成分。例如：
头痛、心疼、目击、性急、地震

（2）翻译下面的词语，看看汉语是哪种形式的复合词

(pop)star _____   marriage _____
remind _____   regret _____
kidnap _____   ban _____
young _____   scream _____
dream _____   witness _____

3. 翻译方法

（1）**省译**(omission)——与"增译"(amplification)相反，"省译"是对原文中的某些词语省而不译。例如（注意英文画线的部分）

a. 介词

① Let the facts speak <u>for</u> themselves.
让事实自己说话。

② last at least 10 minutes <u>at a time</u>
一次至少持续10分钟

③ We are talking <u>about</u> life-saving technology.
我们在谈论挽救生命的技术。

b. 连词

④ Technical inventions traveled faster <u>and</u> further.
技术发明传播得更快、更远。

⑤（His wife Winnie was hounded and harassed for decades,）<u>and</u> his daughters grew up without a father's guidance.

女儿们在没有父亲管教的环境中长大。

⑥ He remains healthy and arises each day at 4∶30 to exercise and eat a traditional South African breakfast of cold porridge and fruit.

他仍然健康,每天4点半起床锻炼,早饭是南非传统的冷麦片粥和水果。

c. 代词

⑦ He changed his mind at last.

他终于改变了主意。

⑧ He has few regrets about his prison years.

对于监狱生活他并不后悔。

⑨ (It must be frustrating to keep hearing how good exercise is for your health.) It needn't be.

没有必要。

⑩ It was John who helped you out of the trouble.

是约翰帮你摆脱了困难。

d. 动词

⑪ The roar of the crowd is deafening.

人们的喊声震耳欲聋。

⑫ He became more and more angry.

他越来越生气了。

⑬ I should get checked regularly.

我应该定期检查。

⑭ He has/feels few regrets about his prison life.

他很少为坐监狱而后悔。

(2) 省译练习(画线的地方考虑省译)

① (after Mrs. Mandela's 1991) conviction for kidnapping

　→

② I can't agree to what you said.

　→

③ (Young girls scream, young men shout his name) and everyone ... pushed closer.

　→

④ (At Fort Hare University,) he met the man who would be his life-long compatriot, Oliver Tambo.
　→

⑤ It is his democratic dream that drives him.
　→

⑥ (The German *Geschwister*, for example,) could be translated as the more concrete and differentiated brothers and sisters or as the more abstract and undifferentiated siblings.
　→

4. 语法练习

(1) **被动句**(passive)

汉语表示被动常见的形式有"N_1 被 N_2 ＋ VP"。例如：
① The ANC was banned by the white government in 1960.
　　1960年ANC被白人政府取缔了。
② His body was spotted by rescuers on Monday.
　　他的尸体星期一被营救人员发现了。
英语被动句"by N_2"经常省略，但是汉语的"被"不一定能省。例如：
③ Mandela was arrested.
　　曼德拉被逮捕了。
④ He is treated like a pop star.
　　他被当作大众明星。
③、④译句的"被"不能省略，因为"曼德拉逮捕""他当作……"可以理解成 Mandela arrested (someone)、he took (something as...)。
　上面这些"被"字句表示消极(adversity)的事情，如①、②；或者受到的对待、处置(disposal)，如③、④(曼德拉被逮捕 the police arrested him；他被当作大众明星 people treat him as a pop star)。
　有些时候"被"可以不用。例如：
⑤ The alien speech is at once rendered into perfect American English.
　　外星人的话立刻(被)转换成标准的美国英语。
⑥ This method is often used to improve the patients' memory.

这种方法常(被)用来改善病人的记忆力。

⑤、⑥不用"被"意思也很清楚,因为"……话转换成……""……方法用来……"只能理解成"……话被转换成……""……方法被用来……"。

有时一定不能用"被"。例如:

⑦ before a new habit is firmly established

一个新习惯养成之前

⑧ Each new word has to be learned individually.

每个生词都要一个个地学。

⑨ How substances in green tea may be linked to skin-cell rejuvenation.

绿茶中的物质怎么能跟恢复皮肤细胞联系起来呢。

⑩ The finding could one day possibly be applied to anti-aging remedies.

这个发现将来或许可以用在抗衰老治疗上。

⑪ This unhealthy habit must be changed.

这个不健康的习惯一定要克服。

⑦、⑧的动词"养成(establish)""学(learn)"没有明确的主语,它们只是说明 habit 和 new word 的状态(established、learned)。⑧、⑨、⑩、⑪中的动词前都有助动词(auxiliary verb:要、能、可以、一定),有助动词的句子一般不用"被"。

也有的时候"被"是必须用的。例如:

⑫ "Their family" was seen as most supportive.

"家庭"被看作是最主要的支持。

⑬ Job security was thought to be the most important aspect of work.

工作稳定被视为最重要的方面。

⑭ Walking is often underrated as a form of exercise.

作为运动的一种方式,走路常常被低估了。

⑫、⑬、⑭中的动词都是表示主观判断(subjective judgment)的,这样的句子要用"被"。

因为汉语的被动句常有"不幸(adversity)""遭遇(suffer)"的消极含义,所以英语的被动形式经常翻译成汉语的主动(active/positive)形式。例如:

⑮ She was "reassured" that her lesions were benign.

医生一再"保证"她的损伤部分是良性的。

⑯ (Seres comes from the Chinese ssu(丝)silk, and) was transmitted to Europe by the Greeks

希腊人把 Seres(这个名字)传到了欧洲。

⑰ Each area is identified by a keyword.

每个领域都由一个关键词来代表。

⑱ increased energy
　　增长的能量

⑲ a much-loved beverage
　　深受喜爱的饮料

⑮给句子加上主语"医生",⑯把句子变成"把"字句,⑰用"由"来强调主动;⑱、⑲原句里的被动形式定语,译成汉语时都不加"被"。

(2) 翻译下面的句子,看看可以用上面介绍的哪一种方法

① (This latest study shows how) Chemicals—known as alkylamines
　　→

② though their effectiveness has not been scientifically proven
　　→

③ The 700 reasons have been grouped into 70 key areas.
　　→

④ (walking on level ground,) 80 steps per minute would be considered a slow pace
　　→

⑤ The meaning that is translated will be decided by situation and context, not by the dictionary.
　　→

⑥ Tea may be the most commonly consumed drink.
　　→

(3) 动词和"着"—— 动词后的"着"表示持续(progressive)的状态。例如:
Young girls scream, young men shout his name and everyone from small children to the elderly pushed closer to…
尖叫着、叫喊着、向前挤着……

第五课　叱咤风云

（4）看看下面句子里画线的动词能不能带"着"（能带"着"画√，不能带画 ×）：

① Those closest to him say it is his democratic dream that <u>drives</u>（驱使）him. （　　）

② Mandela was arrested while <u>disguised</u> as a chauffeur. （　　）

③ "We <u>stand for</u> majority rule（　　）, but we don't <u>stand for</u> black majority rule（　　）", he <u>reminded</u>（　　） the crowd of 150,000 in Durban.

④ Forcibly, she <u>walked</u> us the seven long, hilly blocks. （　　）

5. 指出并改正译句中的错误

① Women tend to wait for an opportunity to present itself.
　→ 女人倾向于等着为机会到来。

② We are talking about my future.
　→ 我们在谈论关于我的未来。

③ Mandela was elected as president.
　→ 曼德拉选为总统。

④ an armed robber
　→ 一个被武装的盗贼

⑤ There is a United Nations "presence" in Rwanda, represented by Col. Oliver.
　→ 在卢旺达有一个被奥利佛上校代表的联合国人员的存在。

⑥ More than 382,000 people are treated for skin cancer each year.
　→ 每年有 382,000 多人因为皮肤癌被治疗。

⑦ At least 60 to 90 minutes a day may be needed to maintain weight loss.
→ 一天至少60到90分钟被需要维持减肥。

⑧ Where he ascends the speaker's podium, the roar of the crowd is deafening.
→ 当他登上讲台时,人群的叫喊声震耳欲聋着。

6. 讨 论

（1）你认为曼德拉什么方面最值得尊敬？

（2）现在世界上还有一些地方存在着民族冲突（conflict）或其他矛盾,你认为哪些方法可以消除（eliminate）或者缓解（relieve）矛盾冲突。

补充材料（Supplementary Materials）

Hotel Rwanda

In 1994, a million members of the Tutsi tribe were killed by members of the Hutu tribe in a massacre in Rwanda. Paul Rusesabagina is a Hutu, married to a Tutsi named Tatiana. He has been trained in Belgium and runs the four-star Hotel Des Milles Collines in the capital city of Kigali. He does his job very well. He understands that when a general's briefcase is taken for safekeeping, it contains bottles of good scotch when it is returned. He understands that to get the imported beer he needs, a bribe must take place. He understands that his guests are accustomed to luxury, which must be supplied even here in a tiny central African nation wedged against Tanzania, Uganda and the Congo. Do these understandings make him a bad man? Just the opposite. They make him an expert on situational ethics. The result of all the things he knows is that the hotel runs well and everyone is happy.

Then the genocide begins, suddenly, but after a long history. Rwanda's troubles began, as so many African troubles began, when European colonial powers established nations that ignored traditional tribal boundaries. Enemy tribes were forced into the same land. For years in Rwanda under the Belgians, the Tutsis ruled and killed not a few Hutu.

Now the Hutus are in control, and armed troops prowl the nation, killing Tutsis. There is a United Nations "presence" in Rwanda, represented by Col. Oliver. He sees what is happening, informs his superiors, asks for help and intervention, and is ignored. Paul Rusesabagina informs the corporate headquarters in Brussels of the growing tragedy, but the hotel in Kigali is not the chain's greatest concern. Finally it comes down to these two men acting as free-lancers to save more than a thousand lives they have somehow become responsible for.

When "Hotel Rwanda" premiered at Toronto 2004, some reviews criticized the film for focusing on Paul and the colonel, and making little effort to "depict" the genocide as a whole. But director Terry George and writer Keir Pearson have made exactly the correct decision. A film cannot be about a million murders, but it can be about how a few people respond. Paul, as it happens, is a real person, and Col. Oliver is based on one, and "*Hotel Rwanda*" is about what they really did.

(From Roger Ebert, *Chicago Sun-Times*, Dec. 22, 2004)

Notes:
Hotel Rwanda:《卢旺达饭店》(片名)　　Tutsi:图西族人
Hutu:胡图族人　　massacre:大屠杀
Kigali:基加利(卢旺达首都)　　scotch:苏格兰威士忌

问题：
作为饭店经理，保罗是怎样的一个人？

翻译：

① married to a Tutsi named Tatiana

② He has been trained in Belgium.

③ Some reviews criticized the film for focusing on Paul and the colonel, and making little effort to "depict" the genocide as a whole.

Gandhi My Father

1948, India. When the Bombay cops pick up a gravely ill destitute off the streets, they need his father's name in order to admit him to hospital. Why does the dying beggar answer "Mohandas Karamchand Gandhi"?

Much is known about Gandhi's non-violent ideals and the "Quit India" movement he founded which was directly responsible for the British grant of independence to India and the creation of Pakistan. Little is known about his family life. This bio-pic attempts to redress the balance. It traces the disintegrating relationship between the Mahatma or 'Bapu' (father) as he was fondly known, with the eldest of his four sons, Hirilal.

Told in flashback, the film establishes the uneasy tensions in the family's South African sojourn where Gandhi practised as a barrister up to 1915. The patriarch's steely insistence that Hirilal abandon his education and wife Gulab in order to assist him in his fight against the inequitable apartheid system, leads to resentment by the young Hirilal.

Post 1915, the entire family relocates to India where resistance to British imperialism is gaining momentum. Hirilal tries to assert his own independence but he is thwarted by opportunists who use the Gandhi name to establish fraudulent companies and discredit the freedom movement.

The Mahatma publicly disowns his wayward son; Hirilal sinks into alcoholic depression.

Adapted from his stage play of the same name, Feroze Abbas Khan's debut is an exploration of a taboo topic in modern India: the possible demerits of Gandhian idealism. Indeed, the film has already created controversy in India.

The fuss is unwarranted. Made with the co-operation of the surviving Gandhi family, Khan's film frustratingly refuses to take sides and portrays both protagonists as flawed individuals caught up in circumstances beyond their control.

(From Anil Sinanan, *Times Online*, Aug. 2, 2007)

Notes:
Gandhi：甘地 non-violent：非暴力
bio-pic：传记体电影 redress the balance：公平处理、达到平衡
sinks into：沉湎于 alcoholic：酗酒者
stage play：舞台剧

问题：
说说甘地父子的关系。导演是怎样处理这种关系的？

翻译：
① Much is known about his non-violent ideals.
_____

② He is thwarted by opportunists who use Gandhi's name to establish fraudulent companies and discredit the freedom movement.
_____
_____
_____

第六课　要做真正的美国人

The Struggle to Be an All American Girl

□ 课文是一位美国华裔姑娘对童年生活的回忆片段,表现了作者对童年生活和华人世界的复杂情感。

□ 本课学习重点是修饰成分（定语）和复译。

Notes:
1. Chinese school: 中文学校、华校
2. Chinese medicine: 中药
3. public school: 公立学校（中小学）
4. Chinatown: 唐人街、中国城、华埠
5. moc but: 毛笔
6. tacos:（墨西哥）玉米饼、豆卷
7. egg rolls: 蛋卷
8. Cinco de Mayo: 墨西哥独立日

It's still there, the Chinese school on Yale Street where my brother and I used to go....

Every day at 5 p.m., instead of playing with our fourth and fifth grade friends or sneaking out to the empty lot to hunt ghosts and animal bones, my brother and I had to go to Chinese school. No amount of kicking, screaming, or pleading could dissuade my mother, who was solidly determined to have us learn the language of our heritage.

Forcibly, she walked us the seven long, hilly blocks from our home to school, depositing our defiant tearful faces before the stern principal. My only memory of him is that he swayed on his heels like a palm tree, and he always clasped his impatient twitching hands behind his back. I recognized him as a repressed maniacal child killer, and knew that if we ever saw his hands we'd be in big trouble.

We all sat in little chairs in an empty auditorium. The room smelled like Chinese medicine, an imported faraway mustiness, like ancient mothballs or dirty closets. I hated that smell. I favored crisp new scents, like the soft French perfume that my American teacher wore in public school.

The language was a source of embarrassment. More times than not, I had tried to disassociate myself from the nagging loud voice that followed me wherever I wandered in the nearby American supermarket outside Chinatown.

The voice belonged to my grandmother, a fragile woman in her seventies who could out-shout the best of the street vendors. Her Chinese was rhythmless. It was quick, too loud, and was unbeautiful. It was not like the quiet, lilting romance of French or the gentle refinement of the American South. After two years of writing with a mocbut and reciting words with multiples of meanings, I finally was granted a cultural divorce. I was permitted to stop Chinese school.

I thought of myself as multicultural. I preferred tacos to egg rolls; I enjoyed Cinco de Mayo more than Chinese New Year.

At last, I was one of you; I wasn't one of them.

Sadly, I still am.

(选自 Elizabeth Wong,《爱的教训》,西安交通大学出版社,1997)

1. 根据文章内容回答问题

(1) 作者为什么不喜欢去中文学校？

(2) 课文里有形象、声音和味道的描写,请你把它们写在下面。
校长的样子：
奶奶的声音：
教室的味道：

2. 词语翻译练习

(1) 汉语的复合词(compounds)

上一课介绍了并列式(parataxis)、偏正式(adjunct-head)和主谓式(subject-predicate)三种汉语复合词。这里介绍另外三种复合词——动宾式(verb-object)、补充式(verb-complement)和重叠式(reduplication)。

动宾式：前一个成分是动作行为,后面是宾语。例如：
有名、得意、当心、动身、教书、知己

补充式：前一个成分是动作行为,后面是结果。例如：
改善、提高、推广、说明、破坏、接近

重叠式：
爸爸、妈妈、哥哥、姐姐、弟弟、妹妹

（2）翻译下面的词语，看看汉语是哪种形式的复合词

divorce _____ group（v.）_____

promote _____ innovate _____

adventure _____ become _____

define _____ succeed _____

grandmother _____ lie（v.）_____

3. 翻译方法

（1）**复译**（repetition）——为了使译文的表达更加明确，把原文省略的词语、代词所指的内容翻译出来。例如（画线的是复译的部分）：

① No amount of kicking, screaming, or pleading could dissuade my mother, who was solidly determined to have us learn the language of our heritage.

不管我们怎么反抗、尖叫或者请求，都无法使妈妈改变主意，她已经下定决心要我们学习传统语言。

② He arrived in Johnnesburg from the Transkei, where he was raised to be a chief of the Thembu.

他从特兰斯凯到了约翰内斯堡。在特兰斯凯，他被当作坦普族未来的首领来培养。

③ (it doesn't really matter what people think of you, says Renee Edelman,) "It's that you get the job done and deliver results."

"重要的是你完成工作、拿出结果。"

④ Reading makes a full man, conference a ready man, and writing an exact man.

读书使人充实，讨论使人机敏，写作使人准确。

（2）复译练习（画线的部分可考虑复译）

① (This latest study shows how Chemicals—known as alkylamines—which) are commonly present in tea as well as wine, apples, mushrooms, and other sources

→

② he was a moral philosopher rather than a preacher of religious faith

→

③ The pioneering SIA scope helps doctors distinguish malignant moles from benign ones.
　　→

④ (China transmitted to Europe a veritable abundance of discoveries and inventions) which were often received by the West with no clear idea of where they had originated
　　→

⑤ If you see benefits—and most people do
　　→

4. 语法练习

（1）修饰成分（modifiers）：定语（attribution）

a. 定语修饰名词。有的定语和名词之间必须带"的"，有的不能带"的"，多数带不带"的"都可以。

▲必须带"的"的

a1）表示领有（possessive）。如：

① your skills：你的能力

② our heritage：我们的传统

③ 81% of the patients：81%的病人

④ body's immune system：身体的免疫系统

a2）表示特性（characteristic）。如：

⑤ stern principal：严厉的校长

⑥ soft French perfume：柔和的法国香水

⑦ busy week：忙碌的一周

a3）表示时间、地点。如：

⑧ Europe in 18th century：18世纪的欧洲

⑨ the book on the desk：桌上的书

⑩ the supermarket outside Chinatown：唐人街外面的超市

a4）句子（relative clause）+的。如：

⑪ the person who lies：撒谎的人

⑫ the calories you burn：你消耗的卡路里

a5)"形容词重叠(reduplication)＋名词"和"又……又……"形式。如：

⑬ a red apple：红红的苹果

⑭ a very clean room：干干净净的房间

⑮ a quick and precise answer：又快又准确的回答

▶不能带"的"的

a6) 表示职业(occupations)、头衔(titles)等。如：

⑯ professional athlete：职业运动员

⑰ Chinese teacher：汉语老师

⑱ Marketing manager：市场经理

⑲ Ph. D. in Literature：文学博士

a7) 表示比喻的说法。如：

⑳ green industry：绿色产业

㉑ black humor：黑色幽默

㉒ erotic website：色情网站

㉓ fox tail：狐狸尾巴

a8) 一些"单音形容词＋名词"形式。如：

㉔ high/good salary：高工资/高收入

㉕ low price：低物价/低价格

㉖ a good friend：好朋友

㉗ high mountains：高山

a9) 一些"数＋量词＋名词"形式。如：

㉘ three bottles of water：三瓶水

㉙ a period of time：一段时间

㉚ a group of people：一群人

必须带"的"的定语，如果不带"的"，意思就不易理解。如：＊绿绿草、＊撒谎人、＊你能力、＊教室里面桌子。不能带"的"的定语，如果带上"的"，意思或者用法会有变化。如：狐狸尾巴(坏人暴露出来的行为或者想法)：狐狸的尾巴(狐狸长的尾巴)；好朋友：好的朋友(交好的朋友，别交坏的朋友)；女朋友(girl friend)：女的朋友(female friend)；中国朋友(a Chinese friend)：中国的朋友(a friend of China)。

b. 定语的顺序。有时一个名词有几个定语，其顺序一般是：

领属(possessive)→代词→数量→形容词→名词。例如：

㉛ 你们公司→那位→获得奥斯卡奖的→年轻→电影→制片人
　　The young Oscar-winning film producer in your company

㉜ 你昨天买的→那两本→很有意思的→汉语→书
　　The two interesting Chinese books you bought yesterday

一般情况下，带"的"定语在前面，不带"的"的定语在后面。换句话说，如果要省掉定语"的"，应该从后面(右边)的定语开始。例如：

㉝ a new healthy habit：一个新的健康(的)习惯(✓)/一个新健康的习惯(✗)

㉞ a cup of hot fresh orange juice：一杯热的新鲜(的)橙汁(✓)/一杯热新鲜的橙汁(✗)

(2) 翻译练习

a. 翻译下面的短语

① his deepest source of sadness
　　→

② 60 minutes of moderate physical activity
　　→

③ the best known Western names for China
　　→

④ three different values of the "legacy of China"
　　→

⑤ seven long，hilly blocks from our home to school
　　→

⑥ the oldest leader to be elected president
　　→

⑦ a repressed maniacal child killer
　　→

⑧ personal benefits that people gain from learning a language
→

⑨ a traditional South African breakfast of cold porridge and fruit
→

b. 把下面画线的部分译成"定语+名词"的形式

⑩ We all sat in <u>little chairs in an empty auditorium</u>
→

⑪ Here is <u>a plan to help you find the mix of opportunities and activities that will work for you.</u>
→

⑫ But you can enjoy <u>the byproducts of physical activity—increased energy, less stress, feeling fitter and sleeping better.</u>
→

5. 指出并改正译句中的错误

① 700 reasons to learn language
→ 700 个的学习外语理由

② the technical inventions transmitted to Europe
→ 技术的发明传到欧洲

③ recent research into the role of women in society
→ 最近妇女社会角色的调查

④ one striking conclusion to be drawn from this comparison
　　→一个惊人的从这个比较得出的结论

⑤ your awareness of different culture
　　→你认识的不同的文化

⑥ (lack) the resolve to fit sessions of resistance training into your busy week
　　→决心把耐力训练时间安排进你的忙的星期

⑦ (break up the day with) two-minutes walks——for example, to the mailbox
　　→两分钟的步行——比如说,到信箱

⑧ adapting a new healthy habit, or dropping an unhealthy one
　　→适应一个新健康习惯,或者丢掉不健康的一个

⑨ he swayed on his heels like a palm tree
　　→他随着脚后跟摇摆了,好像一棵棕榈树

6. 讨论

(1) 课文中的"我"最后说"At last, I was one of you; I wasn't one of them. Sadly, I still am.",你认为她为什么会感到悲哀?

(2) 你能谈谈生活在不同文化里,或者在学习一种外国语言/文化时的"文化认同(cultural identity)""文化休克(cultural shock)"的体验吗?

Their Stories were Similar to My Own

When I told my mother that I wanted to move to England to work, she burst into tears. I was the youngest of four children and not very fit, mother had nursed me through my childhood. "What will you do if you fall ill on the journey?" I had already called a snakehead in my local town. Although the snakeheads are people smugglers, it was as easy as phoning a travel agent, only more expensive: it would take £15,000 and I could leave tomorrow.

I had seen pictures of London Bridge and the red buses. A friend had made good money. Four months later, in September 1997, my parents relented. We spoke to a neighbor, a snakehead we trusted. He could get me to England for £13,000, roughly the cost of a good house in Jinfen where the average monthly wage was £30. My family would borrow the money from friends and relatives, who would charge me interest on the loan.

I thought I would pay the money back quickly, but the reality would be very different. It took six months to reach Britain. We traveled in a group. In each country we were handed over to a new gang leader who would take us to the new country. In Moscow we stayed for 10 days in a hotel and consumed nothing but beer and instant noodles. In Ukraine we were asleep on a train when the police arrested us; incredibly they let us go. After another month, in a dismal flat in the Czech Republic, we were put in lorries and driven to Holland. When we got off the train at London Liverpool Street I knew my journey was over, I just felt vacant, empty.

It took me six years to pay back my debt. I would work 11 hours a day for ₤150 a week. I was so depressed and homesick that I cried all the time. What had I done? In Jinfen I ran a business moulding gold and silver jewellery; now I was working harder than my friends in China.

At my lowest, I joined the Chinese Christian church in King's Cross, north London. Pastor Lawrence befriended me and persuaded me to take part in Ghosts, a film about the plight of the 23 Chinese cockle pickers who died in Morecambe Bay in 2004. Although I didn't pick cockles, the conditions they had lived in were similar to my own: a bed-sit with mattresses on the floor and paint peeling off the walls. Like them, I used to get racial abuse and once my boss at the factory refused to pay me.

I had never acted before and I was very nervous. I was also a single mother and ashamed. I have a son, Sean, who is now six, but it had taken a lot of courage to tell my parents I was pregnant and only a couple of people knew I had a child. Now I have found friends and support and I am studying English three days a week at a college in Birmingham.

My parents have not seen the film; they are not proud of me. They wish, and I wish, that I had stayed in China. But now that I am settled here, I am determined that our future will be better.

(From Vanessa Jolly, *Sunday Times*, Jun. 24, 2006)

Notes:
snakehead：蛇头、组织偷渡的人
Moscow：莫斯科（俄罗斯首都）
Czech Republic：捷克
Holland：荷兰
Morecambe Bay：莫克姆贝湾，英国海湾，捡拾海贝的地方
racial abuse：种族虐待

问题：
① 你能说说"我"去英国的路线和过程吗？

② 请你说说"我"在英国生活的情况。

翻译：

① I had seen pictures of London Bridge and the red buses.
_____

② We spoke to a neighbor, a snakehead we trusted.
_____

③ He could get me to England for £13,000, roughly the cost of a good house in Jinfen where the average monthly wage was £30.
_____
_____

第七课 冰雪不归路

An Arduous and Determined Trek

□ 在感恩节旅行的归途中,金一家人被困在大雪覆盖的偏僻山路上。课文讲述的是这个不幸的故事。

□ 本课学习重点是修饰成分(状语)、动词短语及时间表达。

The family was traveling home to San Francisco in November 25 after a Thanksgiving trip to Portland. They attempted to take a shortcut, but took a wrong turn and found themselves stranded in snow and lost with their young daughters, Penelope 4, and Sabine, 7 months, on one of Oregon's treacherous backroads, which are rarely plowed during the winter.

Temperatures at night hovered near or below freezing. They ran the heater in their car until it ran out of gas, and then they burned the tires to stay warm and attract attention. The parents ate berries, while feeding the children baby food and crackers. When their meager food supply ran low, Kati Kim, the mother who was nursing the younger child, breast-fed both children. After nine days, hoping to save his wife and children, James Kim, the father of the family left to seek help, promising to return if he did not find anyone.

What Kim encountered searchers would later describe as rugged, steep, snowy terrain with sodden branches, slick rocks, downed trees and poison oak nestled between sheer cliffs. Despite those conditions, authorities said, he covered an estimated eight miles before rescuers found his body in a ravine.

"It seems superhuman to me that he was able to cover that amount of distance given what he had and also that he

Notes:
1. San Francisco:旧金山(美国城市)、三藩市
2. Thanksgiving:感恩节
3. Portland:波特兰(美国城市)
4. Oregon:俄勒冈(美国州名)
5. backroad:乡间道路
6. James Kim:詹姆士·金(丈夫,妻子是Kati Kim)
7. Under-sheriff:副警长

8. headquartered in: 总部设在/位于……
9. front page: 报纸的头版、网站首页
10. CEO: chief executive officer, 总裁、执行总裁

had nine days in the car" Josephine County Under-sheriff Brian Anderson said.

Rescue workers said they had found what they believed was a trail of clues from Kim, including three shirts, a wool sock, a blue girl's skirt and pieces of an Oregon state map. A deputy found a message written on white paper on the road, saying the family had been stuck since the Sunday after Thanksgiving and that two children were in the car. "Please send help," it said.

Kati Kim and the girls were spotted Monday by searchers in a private helicopter hired by the family. They were released Tuesday from a hospital in Grants Pass.

Kim's employer, CNET, headquartered in San Francisco, remade the front page of its web site in his memory Wednesday. "This has been a heart-wrenching experience for everyone involved," CNET CEO Neil Ashe said. "I know that I speak for everyone at CNET networks when I say that James Kim was a hero, and we will miss him greatly."

(根据 NBC、CNN 及 CNET 新闻改写)

1. 根据文章内容回答问题

(1) 这家人是怎么度过前面的九天的？

(2) 金为什么离开妻子和孩子？

(3) 请你列出营救人员发现的金留下的东西。

2. 词语翻译练习

(1) 短语的对应(1)：翻译下面的短语，注意定语的形式

baby food _____ their meager food supply _____
slick rocks _____ a wool sock _____
rescue workers _____ treacherous backroad _____
sheer cliffs _____ the younger child _____
downed trees _____ a heart-wrenching experience _____
a message written on white paper on the road _____

(2) 翻译下面的短语和句子，注意动词的时间特点，必要的地方使用表达时间的词语("了"和"过")

breast-fed（the children）_____
ran out of gas _____
food supply ran low _____
covered an estimated eight miles _____
(When I told my mother that…) she burst into tears _____
He even cracked a joke when he called the friend by telephone. _____
_____
(the message… saying) the family had been stuck since the Sunday after Thanksgiving _____
They attempted to take a shortcut, but took a wrong turn and found themselves stranded in snow and lost with their young daughters. _____

In Moscow we stayed for 10 days in a hotel and consumed nothing but beer and instant noodles. _____
_____

3. 翻译方法

(1) 各类状语的翻译

① He stole, not because he wanted the money but because he liked stealing. 他偷窃不是为了钱，他就是喜欢偷。（转译：把 because… 变成"为了……"）

② The days were short, for it was now December.
   现在是十二月,白日短了。(倒译:把原因 for... 变成一般陈述,更自然一些)
③ When it is wet, the buses are crowded.
   下雨天的公共汽车总是很拥挤。(把时间状语变成定语)
④ As the sun rose, the fog dispersed.
   太阳一升起来,雾就散了。(省译:把时间状语变成连动句)
⑤ There was so much dust that we couldn't see what was happening.
   尘土很大,我们看不清发生了什么事。(省译:不翻译 so... that,表达更自然)
⑥ I tried to be polite, although I didn't like him.
   我虽然不喜欢他,但还是显得很有礼貌。(倒译:更符合汉语的表达习惯)

(2)翻译练习
① They ran the heater in their car until it ran out of gas.
   →

② After nine days, hoping to save his wife and children, James Kim, the father of the family left to seek help, promising to return if he did not find anyone.
   →

③ I was so depressed and homesick that I cried all the time.
   →

④ Then the genocide begins, suddenly, but after a long history.
   →

4. 语法练习

把下面的句子译成汉语
① Four months later, in September 1997, my parents relented.
   →

② I used to get racial abuse and once my boss at the factory refused to pay me.
→

③ I had never acted before and I was very nervous.
→

④ Forcibly, she walked us the seven long, hilly blocks from our home to school.
→

5. 指出并改正译句中的错误

① Though he suffered from tuberculosis in prison, he remains healthy.
→虽然他在监狱里患着肺结核,但是现在很健康。

② He has been trained in Belgium and runs the four-star hotel in the capital city of Kigali.
→他在比利时接受的培训,现在在首都基加利开了一家四星级饭店。

③ Post 1915, the entire family relocates to India.
→1915年以后,整个家庭一直住在了印度。

6. 讨论

(1) 如果你是金,在那样的条件下,你会怎么做?
(2) 你对救援人员采取的措施有什么评价?

补充材料(Supplementary Materials)

Day & Night

His ex-wife had been dead less than 12 hours, her throat slashed while their young children slept nearby. He had been summoned back to Los Angeles by the police to be questioned as a possible suspect in the murder. Still, as O. J. Simpson hurried to the Chicago airport on the morning of June 13, he paused to sign an autograph.

The O. J. Simpson case has become such a public obsession that most people can recite location of the bloody glove, the time Nicole called her mother or the number of stab wounds inflicted on Ronald Goldman. But Simpson remains something of a mystery of his own making. In fact, Simpson lived a double life. The corporate spokesman who drank an occasional beer with Hertz executives was also a hard partyer. Some reporters found, who cruised bars and indulged in drugs and random sex.

At some point, a double life can become too much to bear. It is amazing, given the story that follows, how long Simpson kept up the facade. During 1950s, he was a member of a gang called the Persian Warriors. Simpson liked to hit the local pie company ("My favorite was blackberry," he later said). After he spent a weekend in custody for robbing a liquor store when he was 15, a social worker arranged for him to meet Willie Mays, the baseball star who gave young Simpson an inspirational chat about staying out of trouble. O. J. later said he was more interested by Mays's house, a mansion in an affluent part of town. He also watched with envy and fascination as Mays signed autographs for his fans. "I thought, hey, wouldn't it be great for people to know me and love me and want to come up to me."

His choice of college is revealing. Despite poor grades, Simpson could have won a scholarship to almost any state football factory, but he chose the University of Southern California. The school had a higher television profile than most, in part because of its regular appearances in the Rose Bowl. USC also had strong connection to Hollywood. The assistant coach who recruited Simpson, Marvin Goux, was also a bit-part actor who could get O. J. a summer job as an extra at a studio…

Simpson had a strict double standard on philandering. In an interview in 1968, Marguerite, his ex-wife, described her husband "a beast" who had not allowed other young men to talk to her. He, however, was free to roam…. Simpson met the 18-year-old homecoming princess, Nicole Brown in 1977 while she was waitressing at a Rodeo Drive disco, and they started dating immediately. He separated from Marguerite a year later-about the time he and Nicole began living together. Just as the divorce came through, O. J. and Marguerite's baby daughter, Aaren, drowned in their swimming pool.

By 1992, he was losing his proudest possession, his wife. Fed up with O. J.'s abuse and his womanizing, Nicole left Simpson in March of 1992. While Simpson continued to see other woman, he never stopped wanting Nicole back. On the afternoon of June 12, Simpson went to see one of his daughters in a dance recital, but he did not speak to Nicole, and he was not invited to their celebratory dinner at Mezzaluna. Instead, he got in his Rolls-Royce and drove to McDonald's. What he did over the next few hours will be revealed by a murder trial.

Simpson, who seemed stunned and depressed in the days after the murder, is feeling better, according to a close friend. He even cracked a joke when he called the friend by telephone.

(选自 Even Thomas,《爱的教训》,西安交通大学出版社,1997)

第七课　冰雪不归路

Notes:
Simpson：辛普森（美国棒球明星、电影演员）
Los Angeles：洛杉矶（美国城市）
double life：双重生活
too... to...：太……以至于无法……
University of Southern California：南加州大学（美国）
television profile：电视上镜率
bit-part actor：小角色演员
fed up with：受够了
indulged in：沉湎于
come up to：达到、比得上
Hollywood：好莱坞
interview：采访、访谈（节目）
crack a joke：开玩笑

问题：

① 辛普森的双重生活表现在哪些方面？

② 辛普森为什么选择上南加州大学？

翻译：

① less than 12 hours

② a double life can become too much to bear

③ (She) described her husband "a beast"

④ He had been summoned back to Los Angeles by the police to be questioned as a possible suspect in the murder.

⑤ What he did over the next few hours will be revealed by a murder trial.

第三单元 议论文

Unit 3 Argumentation

学习目标 Learning Goals

主题 Topics	8. 如何看待中国的影响力 　 Tempered View of China's Might 9. 学会成功 　 Learning to Succeed 10. 亚洲的变化 　 Changes in Asia
翻译技能 Skills	◇ 从句的翻译(1);短语的对应(2) 　 译法:正与反(affirmation-negation) ◇ 从句的翻译(2);短语的对应(3):搭配关系 　 译法:拆与合(division-integration) ◇ 段落:关联与一致 　 译法:直译与意译(metaphrase-paraphrase)

第八课　如何看待中国的影响力

Tempered View of China's Might

□《中国震撼世界》获2006年度美国最佳商业图书奖。评委意见是,中国正在改变世界。詹姆斯·金奇的书正好捕捉到这一变化的精华。

□课文是对《中国震撼世界》这本书的评论,学习重点是短语、从句的对应以及翻译中的正反关系。

Notes:
1. James Kynge:詹姆士·金奇,英国《金融时报》前驻华首席记者。
2. Manhattan:曼哈顿(美国纽约市商业区)
3. *The World is Flat*:《世界是平的》,作者 Tom Friedman
4. Dortmund:多特蒙德(德国城市、工矿业中心)
5. US Treasury Secretary:美国财政部长
6. power-plays:争夺权力
7. Lenovo:联想集团
8. TCL:中国公司
9. foreign bidding:海外收购、并购

James Kynge recalls how his wife fed him honey sandwiches in their kitchen to calm his nerves as he worked out how to write a book on China, the country that has fascinated him since he first visited as a student in 1982. That Mr Kynge offered this homely insight in front of an audience of top Manhattan executives after receiving the award last week for best business book of 2006 is a measure of the British author's self-deprecating style.

It is also an indication of how different *China Shakes the World* is from *The World is Flat*, which won last year's Financial Times and Goldman Sachs Business Book of the Year Award. Both books are about important forces sweeping the world of business. Yet while Tom Friedman, author of *The World is Flat*, offers a bullish—and polarising—vision of globalization, Mr. Kynge says he deliberately sought to avoid the straitjacket of polemic, which he feels would have misrepresented the complexity of his topic. As he states in the introduction to the book: "The rise of great powers and their subsequent decline from eminence… can rarely be traced in a simple, linear fashion. They are full of twists and turns, false dawns and deceptive signals."

The book begins, for example, not in China, but in Dortmund, at the site of a Thyssen Krupp steel mill that

10. wafer-thin margins: 微薄的利润	
11. geopolitical: 地缘政治的	
12. top-down: 自上而下的	
13. at odds with: 与……不一致/有冲突	

has just been dismantled, piece by piece, and then shipped to China for reassembly. As a symbol of the threat from China, this is a potent one. As Larry Summers, former US Treasury Secretary, put it in a speech at last week's book award ceremony: "There's a vast world of people in Dusseldorf, in Detroit… who fear the prospect of competing with India and China on cost."

But in person, Mr. Kynge is eager to dispel some of that fear. He understands why the developed world feels threatened—not just directly, by manufacturing competition, but indirectly, by such unintended consequences of growth as pollution—but he also sees clearly the potential benefits of China's rise. Asked to identify some of the forces that have developed since the book was published, he settles on the imminent impact of the Chinese middle class.

Some Chinese developments, while painted as power-plays, are signs of the country's weaknesses, he argues. For instance, many commentators have drawn parallels between Chinese companies' expansion abroad—Lenovo's purchase of IBM's personal computer business, or the acquisition by TCL, an electronics group, of Thomson of France and Schneider of Germany—and corporate Japan's foreign bidding spree in the 1980s. But Mr Kynge says China's bids for foreign companies are mostly defensive: "Manufacturing in China is a brutal market with wafer-thin margins and when these companies go abroad, they need to, because they're being killed at home."

That is a more nuanced vision than the one espoused by Mr Friedman and supporters of an adapt-or-die attitude to globalisation. But Mr. Kynge's view of Chinese expansion is not uniformly rosy. He gives a clear sense, both in his book and in his conversation, that the inexorability of Chinese growth is bound to provoke dangerous geopolitical tensions. China's appetite for natural resources, from oil to iron ore, is "indiscriminate and inarticulate", he says. "I don't see any malevolent intent behind China's moves to places like Sudan and Venezuela and Iran. For the Chinese, it's a simple equation. But if you're sitting in Washington, looking at the Chinese becoming the biggest investor in a place like Sudan, propping up a government that the US regards as a rogue state, then it's highly problematic."

But it pains Mr. Kynge that such clashes dominate the world's headlines.

They represent a top-down view of the country at odds with Mr. Kynge's experience of the Chinese people, whom he describes as being "on a quest for spiritual development as great as their quest for material development."

(From Andrew Hill, *Financial Times*, Nov. 1, 2006)

1. 根据文章内容回答问题

（1）金奇的《中国震撼世界》与弗里德曼的《世界是平的》有何不同？

（2）金奇是怎么看中国的海外扩展的？

2. 词语翻译练习

短语的对应（2）：翻译下面的短语，注意定语、状语的翻译。
his wife fed him honey sandwiches _____
sought to avoid the straitjacket of polemic _____
the developed world feels threatened _____
(steel mill that) has just been dismantled, piece by piece, and then shipped to China for reassembly _____
_____

3. 翻译方法

（1）**反译**（negation）——不同的语言，肯定、否定的概念和表达方式不完全相同。有时译文需要用相反的表达形式（原文"否定"→译文"肯定"/原文"肯定"→译文"否定"），才能更准确地反映原文的意思、更容易让人明白。例如：
原文"否定"→译文"肯定"
① It couldn't better! 好极了！
② These shoes are comfortable rather than pretty. 这双鞋不好看，但是舒服。
③ I don't think that's going to happen. 我认为那样的事情不会发生。
原文"肯定"→译文"否定"
④ Students are still arriving. 学生们还没到齐呢。
⑤ The teacher really has an open mind. 老师真的没有偏见。

⑥ The boat sank off the coast. 船在离海岸不远处沉没了。

（2）反译练习

① He didn't come until yesterday.
→

② This is the last thing I would like to do.
→

③ They never meet without quarreling.
→

④ The team is yet to win a game.
→

⑤ You don't know about him without you have read that book.
→

⑥ Marriage is hard enough without bringing such low expectations into it, isn't it?
→

4. 语法练习

把下面的句子译成汉语

① James Kynge recalls how his wife fed him honey sandwiches in their kitchen to calm his nerves as he worked out how to write a book on China.
→

② Asked to identify some of the forces that have developed since the book was published, he settles on the imminent impact of the Chinese middle class.
→

③ He gives a clear sense, both in his book and in his conversation, that the inexorability of Chinese growth is bound to provoke dangerous geopolitical tensions.
　→

④ But if you're sitting in Washington, looking at the Chinese becoming the biggest investor in a place like Sudan, propping up a government that the US regards as a rogue state, then it's highly problematic.
　→

5. 指出并改正译句中的错误

① The book begins, for example, not in China, but in Dortmund.
→这本书开始,例如,不是在中国,而是在多特蒙德。

② (China, the country that) has fascinated him since he first visited as a student in 1982.
→(中国)让他着迷,自从1982年他作为学生第一次去中国。

③ When these companies go abroad, they need to, because they're being killed at home.
→当这些公司去国外的时候,他们必须去,因为他们在国内活不下去。

6. 讨论

(1) 为什么课文作者认为金奇的观点是"tempered view"?
(2) 介绍一本关于中国的书或者文章,说明作者的主要观点。

补充材料(Supplementary Materials)

Sino-EU Partnership Touches New High

The core areas where Sino-EU cooperation will be significantly strengthened in the next few years are energy conservation and climate change. EU Commission sources said that the EU is committed to cutting greenhouse gas emission by at least 20 percent by 2020, through energy measures in particular. It has also revealed the ambitious target of ensuring that 20 percent of its energy supply comes from renewable energy sources. Besides, 75 percent of the EU's new energy investments will focus on the renewable. "Like the EU, China also has a strong demand to meet its energy-saving objectives, the EU and China now have been devoted to plenty of such projects in these areas, working steadily to address priorities," said Serge Andre Abou, Ambassador of the Delegation of the European Commission to China. As the EU maintains high-standards and efficient technologies in construction, transport and industry, the ambassador hopes to team up with several Chinese ministries, such as the State Environmental Protection Administration and the National Development and Reform Commission, to set up an EU clean energy technology center in China.

(From Yang Cheng, *China Daily*, May 9, 2007)

Notes:

partnership:伙伴关系,合作　　　　　EU Commission:欧盟委员会
be committed to:承诺……,致力于……　energy-saving:节能的
greenhouse gas emission:温室气体排放
State Environmental Protection Administration:(中国)国家环保总局
National Development and Reform Commission:(中国)国家发改委
clean energy:清洁能源

问题：

① 未来几年中欧合作的核心领域有哪些？

② 在环境、能源方面欧盟确立了什么目标？

翻译：

① The core areas where Sino-EU cooperation will be significantly strengthened.

② It has also revealed the ambitious target of ensuring that 20 percent of its energy supply comes from renewable energy sources.

Online Campaign Aims to Rid Forbidden City of Starbucks

One of the most incongruous sights of the globalized age—the Starbucks coffee shop inside Beijing's Forbidden City—could soon be a thing of the past after a furious online campaign. In response to this demonstration of "netizen" power, the palace's guardians have announced plans to review the presence of the coffee shop.

Along with Kentucky Fried Chicken and McDonald's, Xing Ba Ke—the Mandarin name for Seattle-based Starbucks—is immensely popular in China. But the outlet inside the palace has stirred up controversy since it opened in 2000. Despite lowering its profile with the removal of its trademark signboards, the coffee shop faces stronger opposition than ever this week. The trigger was a blog entry posted on Monday by Rui Chenggang, a TV anchorman, who called for a web campaign against the outlet that he said "tramples over Chinese culture".

Starbucks said it had no plans to move. "Starbucks appreciates the deep history and culture of the Forbidden City and has operated in a respectful manner that fits within the environment," Eden Woon, vice-president for greater China, told Reuters. "We have provided a welcome place of rest for thousands of tourists, both Chinese and foreign, for more than six years. We are honored to have the opportunity ... to enhance visitors' museum experience."

(From Jonathan Watts, *The Guardian*, Jan. 19, 2007)

Notes:
campaign：宣传活动　　　　　　　　Forbidden City：故宫、紫禁城
Starbucks：星巴克（咖啡店）　　　　netizen：网民
Kentucky Fried Chicken：肯德基　　McDonald's：麦当劳
low profile：低调　　　　　　　　　blog：博客
greater China：大中华地区　　　　　Reuters：路透社（英国通讯社）

问题：

① 根据这篇短文,对于在故宫开店,星巴克和当地电视主持人各持什么观点?

② 你怎么看星巴克在故宫开店以及引起的争论?

翻译：

① (it) could soon be a thing of the past after a furious online campaign

② But the outlet inside the palace has stirred up controversy since it opened in 2000.

第九课 学会成功

Learning to Succeed

□ 如何在竞争激烈的商业社会获得成功、如何使自己的小本经营发展壮大？本文试图给出答案：知识、学习，只有不断充电，你才能找到自己的发展道路。

□课文的学习重点是短语对应和从句的翻译。

Notes:
1. mug:杯子、笨蛋
2. best seller:畅销书
3. strategically: 从战略上
4. real estate guru:房地产大亨
5. self-improvement: 自我提高
6. educated:受过教育的
7. *The Australian*:《澳大利亚人报》
8. business coach:商务指导、商务顾问
9. start-ups:起步者,创业者
10. Chambers of Commerce:商会

You can't educate mugs. You can lead a horse to water but you can't make it drink. Such criticisms are apt for many people in small business. Traditionally, even for entrepreneurs, small business operators  do not seek out the courses offered at universities to improve their business skills. However, and happily, the small number of small business courses offered around the country, in too small a number of institutions, will undoubtedly create better small business owners out of our current crop of students in the future.

That said, of the 1.1 million businesses out there, most of their owners rely on other sources of education, and in too many cases the amount of educational input on a regular basis is close to zero.

Michael Gerber, who wrote the worldwide best seller E-Myth Revisited—arguably one of the best small business educators ever—has made a distinction between entrepreneurs who work on their businesses and technicians who work in them.

Plumbers, bakers, accountants, hairdressers, journalists, lawyers, doctors and landscapers, to name just a few, are technical people who think they could run a business. However, they work in their business for long hours, as Gerber says: "Doing it. Doing it. Doing it." They work so many hours plying their trade they don't have

time to think strategically to grow their business. Education can help you think strategically.

These people create businesses that are often hard to sell because they rely on the founder. Many of the great businesses of our lifetime, such as McDonald's, came about because the small business owner turned himself into an entrepreneur and stopped flipping burgers.

The likes of John McGrath, the Sydney real estate guru, confesses to devouring business self-improvement books. However, he does not let the educational message wither on the vine.

"I create an action plan to implement any new idea I pick up from a book or a seminar I attend," he said. "I don't like to procrastinate."

The educated small business owner belongs to network groups, buys magazines, hangs out for the Entrepreneur section in *The Australian* and scours small business related websites. They are big book buyers but they read them and they implement what they read.

Lesley Ann Grimoldby, an E-Myth consultant based in the Barossa in South Australia, thinks book-reading business owners have got their act together.

"The most successful small business owners I know are constantly seeking to learn from others and the most accessible way to do this is through reading," she said.

"The best books aren't necessarily business books, they are often self-development books which help them to be a better manager and leader."

In recent times we have seen the spectacular growth of business coaches, but life coaches have also become popular. These can be expensive for start-ups, and so groups such as Business Enterprise Centres can be great for budding entrepreneurs. For serious growers, groups such as Australian Business Limited, the Australian Institute of Company Directors, Chambers of Commerce and employer as well as industry groups can be sources of education and inspiration.

It doesn't matter how you get it, but make sure you are not a mug who ignores the importance of education.

(From Peter Switzer, *The Australian*, Nov. 24, 2006)

第九课　学会成功

1. 根据文章内容回答问题

（1）下面的句子用中文怎么说？

You can lead a horse to water but you can't make it drink. You can't educate mugs.

（2）"受过教育的小业主"(educated small business owners)有什么特点？

（3）课文里所说的"专家"(technicians)是指哪些人？他们与"企业家"(entrepreneurs)有什么分别？

2. 词语翻译练习

短语的对应（3）：搭配关系。翻译下面的短语，注意动词的选择和短语的搭配

seek out（the courses）_____

devour business books _____

seek to learn from others _____

reply on other sources _____

wither on the vine _____

implement what they read _____

turn oneself into an entrepreneur _____

industry groups can be sources of education _____

3. 翻译方法

（1）**分译与合译**(division and integration)——为了使译句的结构简单明了，长句子可以考虑分译。例如：

① but make sure (that) you are not a mug who ignores the importance of education

但是一定要明确：你不是一个笨蛋，不会无视教育的重要性
（或：但是一定要确保你自己不是一个无视教育重要性的笨蛋）

② (to write a book on China,) the country that has fascinated him since he first visited as a student in 1982

自从1982年作为学生首次去中国，这个国家一直让他着迷
（或：这个自从1982年作为学生首次访问以来一直让他着迷的国家）

分译还可以使句子之间的关系更加清楚，如上面的"你不是……，不会……""……首次去中国，这个国家……"。

短句子考虑合译，也是为了使译句结构清楚完整。例如：

③ The likes of John McGrath, the Sydney real estate guru…

像悉尼地产界大亨 John McGrath 这类人……
（或：像 John McGrath——悉尼地产界大亨这类人）

④ (feels threatened)—not just directly, by manufacturing competition, but indirectly, by such unintended consequences of growth

不仅仅是来自制造业竞争的直接威胁，而且也有来自增长的后果造成的间接威胁
（或：不仅仅是直接的、由制造业竞争带来的威胁；而且也有间接的、由增长的后果造成的间接威胁）

(2) 用分译或者合译的方法，把下面的句子译成英语

① I create an action plan to implement any new idea I pick up from a book or a seminar I attend.
→

② Michael Gerber, who wrote the worldwide best seller E-Myth Revisited—arguably one of the best small business educators ever—has made a distinction between entrepreneurs who work on their businesses and technicians who work in them.
→

③ Some Chinese developments, while painted as power-plays, are signs of the country's weaknesses, he argues.
→

第九课　学会成功

4. 语法练习

（1）**复句**（compound sentence）——由于英、汉复句各自的特点，在对译时需考虑语序、分合和转换等问题。例如：

① His wife fed him honey sandwiches in their kitchen to calm his nerves <u>as</u> he worked out how to write a book on China.

<u>当</u>他终于想出怎样写一本关于中国的书时，他的妻子在厨房给他吃蜂蜜三明治，以便让他平静下来。（倒译、分译）

② <u>Yet while</u> Tom Friedman, author of *The World is Flat,* offers a bullish-and polarising-vision of globalization, Mr. Kynge says he deliberately sought to avoid the straitjacket of polemic.

《世界是平的》作者弗里德曼提供了一幅乐观的、两极化的全球化情景，而金奇先生则说，他是有意要避免争论的束缚。（关联词放在后面）

③ You can lead a horse to water <u>but</u> you can't make it drink.

你可以把马拉到河边，但是你却无法使它喝水。（分译）

④ They work <u>so</u> many hours plying their trade (<u>that</u>) they don't have time to think strategically to grow their business.

他们做生意花的时间太多，反而没有时间思考发展战略。（转译：把原来的 so…that… 句式变成了对比句，比用"如此……，以致……"句式更自然）

（2）复句练习

① Many of the great businesses of our lifetime, such as McDonald's, came about because the small business owner turned himself into an entrepreneur and stopped flipping burgers.

→

② the outlet inside the palace has stirred up controversy since it opened in 2000. Despite lowering its profile with the removal of its trademark signboards, the coffee shop faces stronger opposition than ever this week.

→

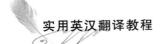

5. 指出并改正译句中的错误

① These people create businesses that are often hard to sell because they rely on the founder.

→这些人经营的生意常常卖不动,由于对创办人的依赖。

② They are big book buyers but they read them and they implement what they read.

→他们买很多书,但是他们读书和实际运用学到的东西。

③ The best books aren't necessarily business books, they are often self-development books which help them to be a better manager and leader.

→最好的书不一定是商业书籍,而它们常常是自我发展的书,这些书帮助他们成为更好的经理和领导。

④ Manufacturing in China is a brutal market with wafer-thin margins and when these companies go abroad, they need to, because they're being killed at home.

→制造业在中国是一个残酷的市场,利润很低,当这些公司向海外发展,它们需要,因为它们在国内很难生存。

6. 讨 论

(1)你认为什么书对你来说最重要?

(2)现在很多大学开办经理培训班,你认为这样的班有用吗?

补充材料(Supplementary Materials)

Pressure of Work Takes Its Toll

Landing a wellpaid job in a foreign company is something millions of China's jobseekers dream of, but the findings of a recent survey may change their minds.

Nearly 90 percent of Chinese staff in foreign companies suffers from work-related illnesses, according to a recent survey by the Horizon Research Consultancy Group. Of the 1,521 respondents working for foreign companies, 91 percent reported symptoms such as burnout, stress, frustration, lack of sleep or numbness in the neck and shoulders after work, said Horizon.

Interviews were carried out over the telephone, via e-mail or fax or face to face in four cities including Beijing, Shanghai, Guangzhou and Wuhan. And 15.4 percent of those surveyed said they suffered from at least seven symptoms, which could lead to a breakdown or serious illness according to Horizon analysts. Another 5 percent said they suffered from at least 10 symptoms, which indicated they were extremely overworked, said Horizon. Half of the respondents said they did little physical exercise, while many complained about working more than 10 hours a day, returning home late at night and having to work over weekends.

Of the most common symptoms of interviewees, 30 percent said they suffered from poor memory, as well as stress, mood swings and accelerated aging. Middle-aged, highly paid employees were more vulnerable to work-related illnesses, according to the survey. A lack of regular health checks and an unhealthy lifestyle, including drinking, smoking and skipping breakfast also made matters worse, according to the survey.

(From Wu jiao, *China Daily*, Feb. 5, 2007)

Notes:
burnout：精疲力竭   interviewee：受访者
skip breakfast：不吃早餐

问题：
① 根据文章的调查，在外企工作的中国员工健康状况怎样，为什么会出现这种情况？

② 说说这些员工有哪些健康问题。

翻译：
Interviews were carried out over the telephone, via e-mail or fax or face to face in four cities including Beijing, Shanghai, Guangzhou and Wuhan.

_____
_____

The Web Redefines Reality

The Internet is something we need only to push a button to get to, something so integrated into our daily lives that it's easy to take for granted. Yet the significance and wonder of the Internet is difficult to overstate.  Our experts shared these points: The Internet is a marvel of modern engineering, with its hyperlinks, routers and fiber-optic cables. It reflects the enlightenment of the modern world. And no human creation in history has connected the world like the Internet.

Our experts also agreed that the Internet can rightfully be called a place—somewhere people "go" to connect to anywhere in the world. Via webcam, they view Seattle from the top of the Space Needle just as easily as they watch rhinos and leopards roam South Africa.

Perhaps the most wondrous thing, though, is how it is redefining the idea of place. In the Internet-based virtual world known as Second Life, for instance, more than 1 million citizens have created representations of themselves known as avatars and have built a place with its own original landscape and currency that can be spent at virtual representations of real world stores, attractions and activities. Want a pair of virtual Adidas shoes? Buy them. Want to see a virtual Duran Duran give a real concert? No problem. Want to crash at a hotel? Try the soon-to-be real-world Aloft Hotel. Small, head-spinning wonders like these pop up every day, and they're all harbingers of things to come.

(From Michael Yessis, *USA Today*, Nov. 15, 2006)

Notes:
redefine：重新界定　　　　　internet：互联网
integrate into：融进、结合　　take for granted：信以为真、认为理所当然
virtual：虚拟的　　　　　　　crash：住宿

问题：
① 根据上面的短文,网络为什么会对我们产生如此巨大的影响?

② 你是怎么看待网络的影响的?

翻译：
① something so integrated into our daily lives that it's easy to take for granted

② In the Internet-based virtual world known as Second Life, for instance, more than 1 million citizens have created representations of themselves known as avatars and have built a place with its own original landscape and currency that can be spent at virtual representations of real world stores, attractions and activities.

第十课　亚洲的变化

Changes in Asia

□ 本文选自联合国《世界文化报告2000》。文章介绍日本"电通人类研究会"1996年开展的一项调查：亚洲六大城市在价值观方面的共性和差异；结论发人深省。

□ 课文叙议结合，观点简明扼要；学习重点包括词语选择、关联和比较。

Notes:

1. Dentsu Institute for Human Studies: 电通人类研究会
2. Tokyo: 东京（日本）
3. Bangkok: 曼谷（泰国）
4. Beijing: 北京（中国）
5. Bombay: 孟买（印度）
6. Jakarta: 雅加达（印尼）
7. Singapore: 新加坡
8. common ground: 共同点、共性
9. come to light: 被发现、表现出来
10. welfare state: 福利国家
11. collective policy arrangements: 集体协商政策
12. follow-up: 后续的、随后的

In 1996 the Japanese Dentsu Institute for Human Studies con-ducted a comparative analysis of global values. Representative samples of citizens from Tokyo, Bangkok, Beijing, Bombay, Jakarta and Singapore were inter-viewed. The Institute reported its first findings in *Tokyo and five other Asian Cities: Diversity and Common Ground*. The last words of the title in particular—common ground—seemed to indicate common changes.

Much of the common ground could be found in the ideas about good health and having good human relationships on the whole and positive ones within the family. These were thought in all the countries to be the most important values. Financial wealth and ambition were only slightly less favored. The same went for values such as convenience, comfort and success at work.

It is perhaps not surprising that people thought of all these things as almost equally desirable. Some interesting diversity came to light, however, when the questioning went into greater detail. Respondents were asked to enumerate their three favorite ways of spending time during the coming five years. Some 26% of the Japanese wanted to spend their time on their jobs. Surprisingly, this percentage was the lowest in the series, with 60% for China (Beijing) the highest. When it came to spending time on hobbies and leisure, 70% of the Japanese felt inclined to give these priority, against 14% of the Indonesians and 5% of the Indians. Dentsu concluded that the Japanese had become more oriented towards leisure and play and that their traditionally high professional orientation had weakened, especially among the younger generation. One might say that in these respects China differs fairly sharply from Japan. It is remarkable that the Chinese seemed to take intellectual effort very seriously: 38% considered taking classes and learning as something to do in the next five years, while 42% thought studying in general was important.

Could ideas about the family and on the roles of men and women still be called traditional? Not necessarily. In all five cities a majority of respondents favored the idea that the roles of men and women should be left to individuals to decide, as opposed to the view that men should do professional work and women should take care of the home. Freedom of choice was also favored in the case of having children. On four out of five countries it was thought that married couples should be able to decide whether or not they would have children.

Nevertheless, traditional opinions on the family were also found. About two-thirds thought that children should look after their parents in old age. This feeling was somewhat weaker in Indonesia (57%), while Japan proved to be a notable exception with only 15%.

It is not so easy to place sacrifices for children's education between the contrasting concepts of tradition and modernity. People took this consideration to heart. Only small categories—generally less than 10%—felt they should not invest heavily in studies. Between 60% and 80% favored the proposal that money should be available for education even if this meant financial difficulties for parents.

In the realm of government some type of welfare state was preferred to individualism and market ideology. A society with full social benefits was preferred to a system featuring low taxes and individual autonomy. Improving the living by market regulation was preferred to an approach based on free competition. Personal freedom should be restricted if it is in the public interest. Half to two-thirds of the respondents supported collective policy arrangements. The Japanese differed from the Asians in one respect. They found it difficult to choose between the regulation of individual rights and fewer rules and more personal freedom.

Democracy was supported. Only small minorities wanted a strong leader to carry out rapid social reform. This wish was strongest in Bombay (35%) and weakest in Japan (5%). The percentages of the other cities ranged from 11% to 18%. The majority of the respondents were of the opinion that the wishes of citizens should be reflected in government policy. The Japanese in particular doubted whether their government would heed their wishes. In a <u>follow-up</u> survey conducted in 1997 it appeared that only 14% of the Japanese believed that the political system truly reflected the will of the people. Compared to European cities, this percentage was significantly low.

The Dentsu findings suggest that new, more individualistic family values seem to be taking hold in Asia. As to a more relaxed attitude to work, the Japanese example appears to be of some relevance. Democracy is an important value. The same applies to the welfare state, which is not in contradiction with Asian values. A certain measure of cultural change can be discerned. So far, the full adoption of societal solutions common to Europe and the United States is supported by minorities only. It would appear that Asian countries are taking over elements of Western culture which they like or can easily incorporate into their own society. The principle of selection leading to diversity would appear to be as important as the tendency towards cultural unity.

(From Jos W Becker, *World Culture Report* 2000, UNESCO Press, 2000)

1. 根据文章内容回答问题

(1)"电通人类研究会"的调查主要目的是什么?

(2)调查发现的共性主要在哪些方面?

(3)调查的主要结论是什么?

2. 词语翻译练习

（1）翻译下面的词语

global value _____

(samples were) interviewed _____

all available means _____

global warming _____

a job interview _____

(money should be) available for _____

（2）翻译下面的数量短语

four out of five countries _____

two-thirds _____

half to two-thirds of the respondents _____

less than 10% _____

（3）为画线的词语选择合适的翻译

married couples（已婚、结过婚、结婚了）

conducted a comparative analysis（指导、开展、管理）

the Institute reported its first findings（第一个、第一次、第一批）

relaxed attitude to work（放松的、随意的、不严格的）

financial wealth and ambition（野心、雄心、奢望）

good human relationships（良好的、优秀的、愉快的）

(the Dentsu findings) suggest that...（显示、建议、提出）

freedom of choice was also favored in the case of having children（拥有孩子、生儿育女、培养孩子）

it is perhaps not surprising that...（惊人的、令人吃惊、感到惊讶）

3. 翻译方法

（1）Much of the common ground could be found in the ideas about good health and having good human relationships on the whole and positive ones within the family.

——大多数共同点存在于对身体健康、总体上拥有良好的人际关系以及积极的家庭关系的看法上。

本句采用了:

(a) 转译,"... could be found in..."译为主动形式"……存在于……"。

(b) 倒译,"... the ideas about..."译为"……对……的看法"。"having good human relationships on the whole"译为"总体上拥有良好的人际关系"。"良好"一般用来描述某种状态,如良好的(国家/个人)关系/(国家/个人)关系良好、良好的身体(心理/精神)状态/身体(心理/精神)状态良好、良好的成绩/成绩良好、良好的表现(记录)/表现(记录)良好。

(c) 复译,"positive ones within the family"译为"积极的家庭关系"。

(2) 说明下面的句子采用了哪些翻译方法

① Financial wealth and ambition were only slightly less favored.

良好的财务状况和雄心壮志受欢迎的程度略次于(这些价值观)。

② It is perhaps not surprising that people thought of all these things as almost equally desirable.

人们对这些方面几乎同样向往,这也许并不令人吃惊。

③ One might say that in these respects China differs fairly sharply from Japan.

人们可能倾向于认为,在这些方面中国与日本有很大的不同。

④ In the realm of government some type of welfare state was preferred to individualism and market ideology.

在政府领域,某种类型的福利社会较之个人主义和市场意识形态更受欢迎。

⑤ Improving the living by market regulation was preferred to an approach based on free competition.

比起自由竞争的方式,通过市场规范提高生活水平更受欢迎。

⑥ They found it difficult to choose between the regulation of individual rights and fewer rules and more personal freedom.

他们在规范个人权利与"少些规定、多些个人自由"之间难以取舍。

⑦ The principle of selection leading to diversity would appear to be as important as the tendency towards cultural unity.

能够带来多样化的选择原则,与文化一致性的倾向看来是同等重要的。

4. 语法练习

(1)"而"的作用

a. When it came to spending time on hobbies and leisure, 70% of the Japanese felt inclined to give these priority, against 14% of the Indonesians and 5% of the Indians.

——在业余爱好和消遣/休闲上花些时间是70%的日本人的优先选择;而印度尼西亚的比例为14%,印度则只有5%。

这里"而…(则)…"表示前后两个方面的不同、差别。再如:

① This wish was strongest in Bombay(35%)and weakest in Japan (5%).

这种愿望在孟买最强(35%),而在日本最弱(5%)。

b. (It is remarkable that the Chinese seemed to take intellectual effort very seriously:) 38% considered taking classes and learning as something to do in the next five years, while 42% thought studying in general was important.

——38%的人考虑在未来的五年中参加学习,而42%的人认为学习总的来说是重要的。

这里的"而"表示前后两个方面的一致性(consistency),再如:

② I did not answer, and he, too, kept silent.

我没有回答,而他也不作声。

③ Things were getting worse in the North, while it was not any better in the South.

北方的情况越来越糟,而南方的情况也好不到哪儿去。

c. This feeling was somewhat weaker in Indonesia (57%), while Japan proved to be a notable exception with only 15%.

——有这种想法的人在印度尼西亚比较少(57%),而日本则只有15%,是一个明显的例外。

这里的"而"表示前后两个方面具有同样的性质,但是后者更甚。再如:

④ Mary was late, and John didn't come at all.

玛丽迟到了,**而**约翰干脆没来。

⑤ He used to eat a little fish, now he is a strict vegetarian.

过去他还吃点鱼,**而**现在则完全吃素食了。

(2) 翻译下面的句子

① People used to believe men should do professional work and women should take care of the home.

→

② Dentsu concluded that the Japanese had become more oriented towards leisure and play and that their traditionally high professional orientation had weakened, especially among the younger generation.

→

③ It is Mrs. White that makes the decisions in that family, not her meek husband.

→

④ All he said was a story,(and)I took his word for it.

→

⑤ We trusted him and he never let us down.

→

⑥ This project caused not prosperity but ruin.

→

⑦ Sally was amused, but I was very embarrassed.

→

⑧ The weather here is chilly in winter, and broiling in summer.
　→

⑨ Those must be comfortable shoes. I bet you could walk all day in shoes like that and not feel a thing.
　→

⑩ This house has wide-open spaces, friendly natives, and spacious dwellings. And it's all within your price range. It's almost too good to be true.
　→

⑪ I was fourteen when I first came to this city. My mom had just killed herself and my step-dad was back in prison.
　→

（3）表示比较

a. 与……相比/比起……(来)/较之……

① Some type of welfare state was preferred to individualism and market ideology.
　与个人主义和市场意识形态**相比**，某种类型的社会福利体制更受欢迎。
　比起个人主义和市场意识形态（**来**），某种类型的社会福利体制更受欢迎。
　较之个人主义和市场意识形态，某种类型的社会福利体制更受欢迎。

② Compared to European cities, this percentage was significantly low.
　与欧洲城市**相比**，这个比例是非常低的。
　比起欧洲城市（**来**），这个比例是非常低的。
　较之欧洲城市，这个比例是非常低的。

b. ……于/更……

③ Financial wealth and ambition were only slightly less favored.
　良好的财务状况和雄心壮志受欢迎的程度则**略逊于**这些价值观。

④ Dentsu concluded that the Japanese had become more oriented towards leisure and play.
　电通的结论认为，日本人已经变得**更**倾向于休闲和玩乐。

⑤ This feeling was somewhat weaker in Indonesia.
这种想法在印度尼西亚要弱**一些**。

c. 最……
⑥ This percentage was the lowest in the series.
这个比例在整个系列中是**最低**的。
⑦ This wish was strongest in Bombay (35%) and weakest in Japan.
这种愿望在孟买**最强**(35%)而在日本**最弱**。

d. 关联(correlation)和一致(consistency)：比较涉及两个或更多的事物。因此，表示比较的词语往往具有关联性，如 same、similarly、more、less、and、but、while 等。翻译时可以采用"分译"的方法，把相关的部分独立出来，放在句首，使其关联作用更加突出。例如：
⑧ These were thought in all the countries to be the most important values. Financial wealth and ambition were only slightly less favored. The same went for values such as convenience, comfort and success at work.
所有国家的受访者都把这些看作是最重要的东西。<u>仅次于这些的</u>，是经济上的良好状况和雄心壮志。<u>同样受到重视的</u>，还有工作上的方便、舒心和成功。

(4) 翻译下面的句子
① She is a better athlete than I.
→

② This pair of shoes fit me better.
→

③ I think I know you better than anybody else.
→

④ A poor spirit is poorer than a poor purse.
→

⑤ Which of these two dresses do you prefer?
→

⑥ Although the pay was as good as the he got previously, the new job gave him more time to stay at home.
→

⑦ Learning makes the wise wiser and the fool more foolish.
→

⑧ Worse than all, rubbishy commercials and harmful programmes lead to bad tastes and a distorted viewpoint towards human life.
→

⑨ Those who know the least of others think the highest of themselves.
→

⑩ Improving the living by market regulation was preferred to an approach based on free competition.
→

5. 指出并改正译句中的错误

① He is better, though not yet cured.
→他更好了,不过还没痊愈。

② This pair of shoes fit me better.
→这双鞋子合我的脚好一点。

③ She was 23 and newly married, a law student about to start a summer job.
→她是一个 23 岁的法律专业学生而刚刚结婚,正要开始做一份暑假工作。

④ This wish was strongest in Bombay and weakest in Japan.
→这种愿望在孟买最强而且在日本最弱。

⑤ Like the EU, China also has a strong demand to meet its energy-saving objectives.
→好像欧盟一样,中国也有满足节能目标的重大要求。

⑥ I think I know you better than anybody else.
→我想我更了解你比别的人。

⑦ Readers joined some authors in a plea to J.K. Rowling not to kill off Harry Potter in the seventh and final book.
→读者也一些作家联合请求J.K.罗琳不要在第七部,也就是最后一部书中杀死哈利·波特。

⑧ But much less interest has been shown here at home in the Chinese language and literature than either of those countries.
→但是在国内,对于中国语言文学所表现的兴趣,比较那两个国家来要少得多。

6. 讨论

(1) 如果有更多的时间,你认为应该花在工作上,还是应该花在休闲和爱好上?

(2) 你认为,解决亚洲存在的社会问题能不能完全采用欧美通用的模式?

Times Atlas Shows Effect of Global Warming

The drastic effects of climate change across the globe are disclosed in a new world atlas

Cartographers of the Times Comprehensive Atlas of the World have had to redraw coastlines and reclassify land types because of the effects of global warming. Since the atlas was last published four years ago, sea levels have lowered in some cases and risen in others while ice caps have shrunk and lakes have almost disappeared.

The atlas's editor-in-chief, Mick Ashworth, said: "We can literally see environmental disasters unfolding before our eyes. We have a real fear that in the near future famous geographical features will disappear forever." The main culprits, he added, are climate change and ill-conceived irrigation projects. Some of the changes include:

- The Aral Sea in Central Asia has shrunk by 75% since 1967.
- Lake Chad in Africa has shrunk by 95% since 1963.
- The Dead Sea is 25m lower—the height of five double-decker buses—than it was 50 years ago.
- Sections of the Rio Grande, Yellow, Colorado and Tigris rivers are now drying out each summer. At some times of the year they fail to reach the sea.
- The Bangladesh coastline has had to be withdrawn as more land is lost to the sea as a result of heavier monsoons and rising sea levels.
- Mount Kilimanjaro in Africa has lost more than 80% of its ice cap in the last 100 years.

- The Pacific islands of Kiribati, Marshall Islands, Tokelau, Tuvalu and Vanuata are all under serious threat from rising sea levels.

Urbanization

The Atlas claims that the world population is becoming increasingly urbanized and that within the next year people living in towns and cities will outnumber those living in rural areas for the first time.

- In the 100 years up to 1950 the greatest population shifts took place in Europe and North America but in the last 50 years there has been a massive growth in the number of urban dwellers in the less developed countries.
- By 2030 three in five people (59.9%) will be urbanites and the global urban population is expected to grow to 4.9B. It was 1.3B in 1970.
- Between 2010 and 2030 Africa and Asia are expected to account for five out of every six of the world's new urbanites.
- In 1950 only New York had over 10m inhabitants now there are 18 cities of this size.
- By 2015 there are expected to be 22 including Africa's first "megacities"—Lagos and Cairo.

Good news

- 13% of the world's land surface is now within over 107,000 designated protected areas worldwide.
- The world's wind power capacity increased by more than 20% between 2004-2005.
- Large areas of the Mesopotamian Marshlands in Iraq—drained by Saddam Hussein—are being reflooded.
- A dam has been built to stop water flowing out of the rapidly shrinking Northern Aral Sea causing levels to rise. The fishing industry is reviving, diets have improved and people are healthier.

- This year 22 new sites were added to UNESCO's World Heritage list of outstanding cultural and natural sites including the Sydney Opera House and the Old Town of Corfu bringing the total to 851.

(From Paul Eccleston, *Daily Telegraph*, Sep. 3, 2007)

Notes:
Comprehensive Atlas of the World：世界地图全集
global warming：全球变暖　　　　sea level：海平面
editor-in-chief：主编　　　　　　　Aral Sea：咸海
Bangladesh：孟加拉　　　　　　　Pacific：太平洋
urbanization：城市化　　　　　　　three in five：五分之三
UNESCO：联合国教科文组织　　　World Heritage list：世界遗产名录

问题：

① 根据地图册主编的话，地貌变化的主要原因是什么？

② 文章所说的"好消息"包括哪几个方面？

翻译：

① in the near future
_____

② unfolding before our eyes
_____

③ We have a real fear that…
_____

④ Since the atlas was last published four years ago, sea levels have lowered in some cases and risen in others.
_____

⑤ The Dead Sea is 25m lower—the height of five double-decker buses—than it was 50 years ago.
_____

⑥ A dam has been built to stop water flowing out of the rapidly shrinking Northern Aral Sea causing levels to rise.

第四单元　应用文

Unit 4　Practical Writing

学习目标 Learning Goals

主题 Topics	11. 招生、就业与住房 　　Admission, Employment and Residential 12. 休闲与娱乐 　　Leisure and Entertainment
翻译技能 Skills	◇ 介词和相关搭配 　　特殊表达的翻译 ◇ 词语的语体色彩和感情色彩

第十一课 招生、就业与住房

Admission, Employment and Residential

Admissions Requirements

Admission to the Walton MBA Program requires the completion of our online application, as well as the following components, each of which is explained in greater detail on the application:

Background Information Background information includes: Contact information (e.g. mailing address and phone number), date of birth, academic degrees earned, professional experience and family information.

Two Letters of Recommendation The Admissions Committee requires two recommendations from professional supervisors who are familiar with your work. Optimal sources for recommendations are your direct managers, who can give insight to the Committee on you as an employee. Other useful sources are clients or former employers.

Three Essays All the essay questions have fields large enough for you to answer each question thoroughly. The equivalent of approximately 1-3 pages (250-750 words) is a general range.

Transcripts Applicants to the Walton MBA Program must arrange to have official transcripts sent from their prior academic institutions in time to be received by the February 1 deadline. The Admissions Committee must receive an official transcript before a decision can be made.

Interviews You should schedule an interview before the

□ 本课选自工商管理硕士课程的招生简章，包括录取条件和报名资格。课文在行文和格式上具有招生简章的一般特点，适用于其他专业。

□ 本课的学习重点是介词及其搭配、特殊表达的翻译。

Notes:
1. transcripts：成绩单
2. deadline：截止日期
3. interview：面试
4. non-refundable：不予退还的
5. regarding：对于
6. endorsement：批准
7. commitment：投入

application deadline of February 1, and you must have completed it by March 1. An early interview is strongly encouraged.

Application Fee A non-refundable application fee of ＄150 must accompany your application.

Candidate Qualifications

While there are no fixed requirements regarding age and work experience, class profile averages typically reflect:

- 8 or more years of work experience
- 5 or more years in a managerial position
- 30 years of age or older
- A college degree or the equivalent
- Senior management experience or potential

All applicants must have the written endorsement of their organization, confirming that the organization supports the application and understands the time commitments required to fulfill all class attendance and study. Traditionally, approximately 70％ of students receive full or partial financial support from their organization. Individuals may finance their own tuition.

1．根据文章内容回答问题

（1）报考沃顿工商管理硕士课程需要提交哪些材料？

（2）招生委员会比较重视什么样的推荐？

（3）从现有学员来看，什么样的人被录取的可能性比较大？

2. 词语翻译练习

(1) 翻译下面的词语

online application _____   contact information _____
mailing address _____   supervisor _____
employer/employee _____   field _____
deadline _____   schedule _____
accompany _____

(2) 翻译下面的短语

as well as _____   in great detail _____
to have sth. sent to _____   be familiar with _____
admission to _____   full financial support _____

(3) 为画线的词语选择合适的翻译：

<u>date of birth</u>（生日、出生日期、生日时间）

<u>academic degree earned</u>（学位所得、所获学位、获得学位）

<u>written</u> endorsement（书写的、写好的、书面）

<u>optimal sources for recommendations</u>

（最满意的推荐来源、最理想的推荐人、提供推荐的最好来源）

<u>8 or more years</u> of work experience（八年以上、八年或者更长时间、八年多）

your <u>direct manager</u>（直接经理人、顶头上司、直接管理者）

3. 翻译方法

(1) 介词短语的翻译

与汉语一样，英语的介词及其短语使用灵活，含义丰富，翻译时需要结合上下文确定其意义和用法，找到适当的汉语对应形式。下表简要归纳了一些常见的对应译法。

汉语 对应表达	英语 介词	例　子
在…… ①表示地点 ②表示时间	at in	① **at** work, women may not steal supplies as often as men 在工作场所，…… 　　I am studying English **at** a college in Birmingham 我在伯明翰的一所学院…… ② detect skin cancer **at** an early stage 在早期检测出皮肤癌 　　**at** some times of the year they fail to reach the sea 在一年中的某些时候，…… ① he has been trained **in** Belgium 他在比利时接受培训 　　currently reside **in** Shanghai 目前居住在上海
在……上 ①表示空间 ②表示…… 方面	in	① the role of women **in** society 女性在社会上的角色 　　published his own study **in** the *Journal of* … 在……刊物上发表了…… ② women are also doing more lying **in** the realm of relationships 在个人关系上/方面 　　there has been a massive growth **in** the number of urban dwellers 在城市居民的数量上……
在……中 ①表示事件 ②表示范围	in of	① **in** an interview in 1968 在1968年的一次采访中 　　**in** a car accident 在一次交通事故中 ② **of** the most common symptoms of interviewees, 30 percent said they suffered from poor memory 在受访者最常见的症状中，…… 　　skin cancers comprise 81 per cent **of** all new cancers diagnosed in Australia annually 在澳大利亚诊断出来的所有新病例中……
在……里 ①表示时间 ②表示空间 ③表示抽象 的空间	in	① **in** the next few years 在接下来的几年里 　　**in** the last 100 years 在过去的一百年里 ② drowned **in** their swimming pool 淹死在他们的游泳池里 　　substances found **in** tea 在茶叶里发现的物质 ③ **in** their personal lives 在个人生活里 　　**in** the film *Man Bites Dog* 在《人咬狗》这部电影里
于…… ①表示时间 ②表示原因 ③表示起作 用的因素	in from on	① born **in** 1961 生于1961年 　　who indulged **in** drugs 沉迷于毒品 ② 1300 die **from** the disease in that time …… 死于这种疾病 ③ depending **on** context and desired effect 取决于情景和想要的效果
从……中 表示从哪 里得到	from	everyone can gain benefits **from** learning a language 从学习语言中得到好处 one striking conclusion to be drawn **from** this comparison is that 从这个比较中得出的惊人结论是……
来自…… 表示从哪里 来	from	Seres comes **from** the Chinese ssu（丝）silk "Seres"来自…… two recommendations **from** professional supervisors 来自上级的推荐信 a designer **from** mainland China 来自中国大陆的设计师

续表

汉语对应表达	英语介词	例　子
到…… 表示物体移动的终点	to	drove **to** McDonald's 开车到麦当劳 exposing blood **to** these chemicals 把血液放到这些化学物质里 Chinese ssu（丝）silk, and was transmitted **to** … 中国丝绸传到……
对…… ①表示行为的对象 ②表示心理活动的对象	to with for	① if someone says **to** you 如果有人对你说 　 In response **to** this demonstration of "netizen" power 对网民力量展示的回应 　 exercise is good **to** your health 锻炼对健康有好处 ② satisfaction **with** one's health 对自己的健康感到满意 　 China's appetite **for** natural resources 对自然资源的渴望
对于…… 表示某种判断的对象	for	**for** the Chinese, it's a simple equation 对于中国人来说，…… such criticisms are apt **for** many people in small business 对于很多从事小生意的人…… these can be expensive **for** start-ups 对于起步者……
往…… 表示目的地	to	Simpson hurried **to** the Chicago airport 辛普森匆忙往机场赶 flight Number CA933 **to** Paris 飞往巴黎的 CA933 班机
跟…… ①表示比较的对象 ②表示共同行为的另一方（可用"与""和"）	to from with	① the conditions they had lived in were similar **to** my own 他们的生活条件跟我的差不多 ② married **to** a Tutsi named Tatiana 跟一个叫塔夏娜的图西族姑娘结了婚 　 we spoke **to** a neighbor 我们跟一位邻居谈 　 he separated **from** Marguerite a year later 跟/与玛格尔利特分居 　 interact confidently **with** people 自信地跟/与别人交流 　 a serial killer is having dinner **with** his friends … 正跟/和朋友们一起吃饭
向…… 表示给予、索取的对象	to from	who can give insight **to** the Committee 向委员会提供深入的看法 submit your full CV and cover letter **to** our HR department 向人力资源部门提交完整的简历 my family would borrow the money **from** friends and relatives 向亲戚朋友借钱
给…… 表示行为的受益、受影响者	for	provided a welcome place of rest **for** thousands of tourists 给成千上万游客…… Mays signed autographs **for** his fans 给影迷签名 the variation between … has two consequences **for** translation 给翻译带来两个结果
以…… 表示方式	in	**in** a respectful manner 以充满敬意的方式 our survey suggests that each is devilish **in** different ways 以不同的方式……

续表

汉语对应表达	英语介词	例　子
用…… 表示手段/凭借	with for	**with** that same nest egg, you can get a slice of prime real estate 用同样的积蓄，你可以…… **for** the same price, you can buy 200,000 acres of prime Sahara wasteland 用同样的钱……
有着…… 表示伴随/存在的状态	with	have built a place **with** its own original landscape and currency 有着自己独特的风景和货币 there is a place **with** wide-open spaces, friendly natives, and spacious dwellings 有着开阔的空间…… the Wudaokou area **with** its student ambience has less flash and dash 有着学生氛围的五道口……
……的 ①表示所占部分或比例 ②表示所属 ③表示行为的对象 ④表示性质与归属 ⑤表示所在	of to in	① 80% **of** those responding 80%的回信人 　71% **of** men vs. 61% women 71%的男性比61%的女性 　the transfer will nearly always involve some form **of** loss or change 某种形式的损失或者改变 ② the vocabulary **of** a foreign language 一种外语的词汇 　they're all harbingers **of** things to come 事情的先兆 ③ his choice **of** college is revealing 他对大学的选择 　an exploration **of** a taboo topic in modern India 对现代印度一个禁忌话题的探索 ④ Admission **to** the Walton MBA Program 沃顿MBA课程的录取 　Applicants **to** the Walton MBA Program 沃顿MBA课程的申请者 ⑤ the corporate headquarters **in** Brussels 布鲁塞尔的联合总部 　a mansion **in** an affluent part of town 城市富人区的一座豪宅
因……（而）…… 表示原因	for	After he spent a weekend in custody **for** robbing a liquor store 因抢劫酒店（而）被监禁 More than 382,000 people are treated **for** skin cancer each year 因皮肤癌（而）接受治疗

除了上表归纳的对应形式外，英语介词短语的翻译有时还可以用下面的翻译方法。

a. 转译。例如：

① distinguish malignant moles <u>from</u> benign ones

　把恶性肿瘤与良性的区别开来（from→与）

②（which）were often received by the West <u>with</u> no clear idea of where they

had originated
　　而不知道它们的来源（with→而）
③ bringing in sales on a consistent basis
　　带来可靠的销售收入（状语→定语）
b. 省译。例如：
④ those closest to him say
　　那些最亲近他的人说
⑤ after receiving the award last week for best business book of 2006
　　2006年最佳商业图书奖
c. 倒译。例如：
⑥ Nicole left Simpson in March of 1992
　　1992年3月尼可离开了辛普森
⑦ so much for the universal translator
　　万能翻译机也不过如此
d. 增译。例如：
⑧ we traveled in a group
　　我们是一群人一起旅行的
⑨ the film was criticized for focusing on violation
　　因突出暴力而受到批评
e. 分译。例如：
⑩ protect the brain from the effects of ageing
　　保护大脑，使其免受老化的影响
⑪ first class facilities with full furniture and electric appliances
　　一流的设施，家具、电器齐全

（2）翻译下面句子画线的部分
① the survey brought out considerable differences in what women hoped to get from their wok.
　→

② Britain women put high priority on employer provision of childcare.
　→

③ Increase the size of one type of defensive response to simulated infection by up to five times.
→

④ USC also had strong connection to Hollywood.
→

⑤ But Simpson remains something of a mystery of his own making.
→

⑥ This would be ideal for students pursuing masters degree or higher.
→

⑦ Some reviews criticized the film for focusing on Paul and the colonel.
→

⑧ Despite lowering its profile with the removal of its trademark signboards.
→

⑨ At my lowest, I joined the Chinese Christian church in King's Cross.
→

⑩ In Britain, flexible working hours were clearly most highly valued, with job security ranking second.
→

⑪ He was not invited to their celebratory dinner.
→

⑫ He also watched with envy and fascination as Mays signed autographs for his fans.
→

4. 特殊表达的翻译

（1）Applicants to the Walton MBA Program must arrange to have official transcripts sent from their prior academic institutions in time to be received by the February 1 deadline.

——沃顿工商管理硕士课程申请者应告知原学校于 2 月 1 日（截止日期）前及时邮寄正式成绩单。

这是招生、招聘简章中常见的表达。原句较长，翻译时尽量保持这种紧凑的风格。主要方法包括：

a. 转译和省译：

arrange to have official transcripts sent from their prior academic institutions
告知原学校邮寄正式成绩单

b. 倒译和转译：

in time to be received by the February 1 deadline
于 2 月 1 日（截止日期）前及时邮寄

c. 正确使用助动词、介词等：

must → 应/须（不是"应该""一定""要"）；by → 于……之前。

d. 词语搭配尽量使用紧缩形式：

申请……的人 → ……申请者；原先的学校 → 原学校

练习

① Candidates must speak fluent English and currently reside in Shanghai or be in a position to relocate immediately upon being offered the position.
→

② Candidate must be proactive, hard working and have good Microsoft office skills and be able to work mornings.
→

（2）8 or more years of work experience
　　　具有八年或八年以上工作经验
　　　30 years of age or older
　　　年龄在 30 岁或 30 岁以上

这也是应用文体中常见的表达。句子较短，结构简省；在翻译过程中既要保持原文风格，也要考虑表达的完整和风格的一致。例如，8 or more years → 八年或八年以上，不应译为"八年或更长"；30 years of age or older 也不应译为"30 岁或者更老"。增加适当的词语可使结构更加完整,如"具有""年龄"。

练习

① 5 or more years in a managerial position

② a college degree or the equivalent

③ senior management experience or potential

④ new 2 bedrooms self catering, in the heart of Beijing city

(3) 招生、招聘等材料中常见名称和中文表达

program	课程、项目	managerial position	管理岗位
academic degree	学位	relocate	搬迁、重新安置
recommendation	推荐信	compensation package	工资待遇
admissions committee	招生委员会	probational period	试用期
tuition	学费	administrative/clerical	办公室工作
class attendance	出勤	part-time work	兼职工作
interview	面试	qualification	资格、条件
contact information	联系方式	consultant	顾问、咨询师
mailing address	通信地址	salary and benefit	工资福利
CV	简历	2 bedroom	两居室、两居
cover letter	申请书、求职信	residential building	住宅楼
work permit	工作许可	interior decoration	内部装修
employee	雇员	facilities	设施
employer	雇主	full furniture	全套家具
HR department	人力资源部	electric appliances	家电
finance division	财务部	real estate	房地产
seminar	演示、研讨会	business trip	出差

5. 讨论

(1) 有人认为最好长期从事一种工作,也有人认为应该经常换工作,你赞同哪种观点?

(2) 在工作或者学习与个人生活发生冲突的时候,你认为哪一个应该优先?

补充材料(Supplementary Materials)

GP Relationship Management / Sales

GP is currently seeking candidates to fill a vital position within our Shanghai finance division. Candidates will learn everything from seeking out potential clients to constructing financial portfolios along side our portfolio research and analysis committee.

Candidates must speak fluent English and currently reside in Shanghai or be in a position to relocate immediately upon being offered the position. A second language is a plus! You must have sales experience, as this will be your primary function.

Financial Consultant Role Includes

- Develop and generate Client leads
- Promote GP's financial services division
- Book appointments with potential Clients
- Conduct meetings with clients and recommend financial products according to their needs and goals
- Responsible for bringing in sales on a consistent basis
- Conduct group seminars and attend monthly dinner events in order to generate referrals efficiently.

What You Can Expect?

Compensation packages are extremely competitive and will be discussed during your interview. Provided you progress through our 3 month probational period, you will receive a one year Z Visa and work permit.

Outstanding Career Progression

This position, through the Career Development Program, will include a fast-track route to a sales management position for those interested.

We invite all candidates to submit your full CV and cover letter to our HR department.

> **Notes:**
> candidate：申请者，候选人   seminar：研讨会
> on-site：现场

问题：

① 你觉得这个工作值得申请吗，为什么？

② 申请者要具备什么样的条件？

翻译：

① Candidates must speak fluent English and currently reside in Shanghai or be in a position to relocate immediately upon being offered the position.

_____

② Compensation packages are extremely competitive and will be discussed during your interview.

_____

Part-time Admin Assistant

Company	The DT Group
Status	Part Time, Employee
Occupations	Administrative Support
Industry	Employment Agencies
Location	Los Angeles, LA20011
Job Category	Administrative/Clerical
Career Level	Experienced (Non-Manager)
Education Level	Bachelor's Degree

Job Description

- Calling out students pursuing higher education looking for part time work
- It's every day for morning hours (approx 8:30 am to 12:00 am)

- We currently have two openings that we are actively looking to fill for a top Investment Bank!
- Candidate must be proactive, hard working and have good Microsoft office skills and be able to work mornings
- This would be ideal for students pursuing masters degree or higher!

Job Responsibilities
- Provide administrative support
- Spreadsheet/Data Entry
- Filing (both physically and electronically)

Job Qualifications
- Bachelor's degree or higher
- Previous office experience

Salary and Benefits
$17/hr

Contact Information
Company: The DT Group
Email: ABC@dt-la.com
Reference Code: ABC-PTEE

问题：

① 你觉得学生做兼职工作利大还是弊大？

② 这个工作适合你做吗？

翻译：

① Candidate must be proactive, hard working and have good Microsoft office skills and be able to work mornings

_____

② Provide administrative support

_____

③ Filing (both physically and electronically)
_____

④ Previous office experience
_____

Beijing Apartment Rental

New 2 bedrooms self catering, in the heart of Beijing city, very close to Tian'an Men Square, Temple of Heaven, subway line 5 and 2.

2 bedroom, 1 bathroom, sleeps 4-5 people.

Price range: £40-100 per day

Vacation Rental Description

Brand new pure residential building, located right in the heart of Beijing, very close to Tian'an Men Square, Temple of Heaven, subway line 2 Chongwen Men and line 5 Ciqikou. Entirely new & excellent interior decoration. First class facilities with full furniture and electric appliances. In short if you are looking for a great place to come and stay in this wonderful and ancient city then look no further. Contact me at zbjzf@gmail.com.

Activities near Beijing

Children's playground, cinema, Gym, night club, restaurant, shopping, theatre.

Facilities in the Apartment

Air conditioning, cable or satellite television, cooking utensils, elevator, heating, kitchen, linen service, microwave, parking, refrigerator, TV, washing machine.

Apartment Rental Rates

Low season price: £40 per day

High season price: £100 per day

第十一课 招生、就业与住房

问题：

① 什么样人的适合租住这个房子？

② 你关心的什么问题这个广告没有说到？

翻译：

① new 2 bedrooms self catering

② brand new pure residential building, located right in the heart of Beijing

③ first class facilities with full furniture and electric appliances

Duplex

So, you're finally settling down. You've saved up a little nest egg and are ready to dive into the real estate market. Let's do a little shopping around.

The American dream home, two bedrooms, two bathrooms, one doghouse, one garage, two garbage cans. It's cozy, safe, and just barely within your overstretched budget.

Not for you? For the same price, you can buy 200,000 acres of prime Sahara wasteland. Put up a cottage. Nothing, but you and the sky. It's like a beach without the ocean.

Too remote? Oh, I understand. You need the thrill and excitement of the big city. With that same nest egg, you can get a slice of prime real estate. Not this real estate. Cozy and affordable, this lovely fixer-upper is the perfect place for a dynamic couple like you. No need to putter around the house. It's all right there where you stand.

What's the matter? Feeling a little cramped? Well, just a stone's throw away, just one bridge or a tunnel ride, just outside the big, bustling city, there is a place with wide-open spaces, friendly natives, and spacious dwellings. And it's all within your price range. It's almost too good to be true.

问题:

① 这个说话的人用了什么方法说明这个房子的好处?

② 你听了以后感到困惑吗? 为什么?

翻译:

① For the same price, you can buy 200,000 acres of prime Sahara wasteland.

② Cozy and affordable, this lovely fixer-upper is the perfect place for a dynamic couple like you.

第十二课 休闲与娱乐

Leisure and Entertainment

A Tour to Guilin

Tour Itinerary

☆ Day 1: Arrive in Guilin. Airport or Railway Station pick-up and trans-fer to hotel accom-modation.

- 中国有"桂林山水甲天下"的说法,很多外国游客也热爱桂林的如诗如画、阳朔的自然意趣。这篇课文给你介绍一个"桂林四日游"。

- 本课的学习重点是词语的语体色彩和感情色彩。

☆ Day 2: Guilin (Breakfast/Lunch/Dinner)
A city sightseeing to Elephant Trunk Hill, Seven Star Park, Reed Flute Cave, Diecai Mountain.

☆ Day 3: Yangshuo (Breakfast/Lunch/Dinner)
After breakfast, a cruise along the Li River to the town of Yangshuo carries us through this magical landscape, and visit the famous: West Street of Yangshuo, then go to Longsheng, stay in Longsheng Para-Para Hotel.

☆ Day 4: Longsheng (Breakfast/Lunch)
After breakfast, visit Longsheng Dragon's Backbone Rice Terraces and Hot Spring National Park, then go back to Guilin. End of the tour, then transfer to the Airport or Railway Station.

Notes:

1. pick-up:接人,接……走
2. Elephant Trunk Hill:象鼻山
3. Seven Star Park:七星公园
4. Reed Flute Cave:芦笛岩洞
5. Diecai Mountain:叠彩山
6. Li River:漓江
7. Longsheng:龙胜(温泉)
8. Dragon's Backbone Rice Terraces:龙脊梯田
9. van:面包车
10. admission ticket:门票

Hotel	Number of adults	Tour Price	Single Room Supplement
5 star	2—3	USD480/adult	USD140
4 star	2—3	USD440/adult	USD110
3 star	2—3	USD390/adult	USD80

Price Includes

1. Car or van transportation in each city.
2. All admission tickets, English speaking guide service.
3. Daily breakfast at the hotel, Chinese lunch and dinner are offered outside the hotel or as specified in the itinerary.
4. Travel Agencies' Liability Insurance with the tour inside China.

Price Excludes

1. Gratitude to guide and driver is not included.
2. Expenses of a personal nature such as laundry, drinks, telex, telephone calls or overweight baggage charges.

Chinese Breakfast

- Dumplings (6) (meat or vegetable)
- Soup or fried noodles (meat or vegetable)
- Fish porridge
- Chicken porridge
- Pork & preserved egg porridge
- Ground beef porridge
- Pan fried ricesheet roll
- Pan fried noodle
- Chinese doughnut
- Green tea (free)

From 7:30 AM to 11:00 AM, $4.5 each

No food or drinks from outside. Thank you!

1. 根据文章内容回答问题

(1) "桂林四日游"当中你喜欢哪一天的行程？

(2) 下面哪一项是不包括在"四日游"费用中的：交通、小费、门票、洗衣、保险、行李超重、电话、早餐？

（3）课文里的中式早餐你吃过哪些？你喜欢中式早餐吗？

2. 词语翻译练习

（1）翻译下面的词语

accommodation _____   sightseeing _____
specified _____   expenses _____
charge _____   insurance _____

（2）翻译下面的短语

tour itinerary _____   national park _____
go back to Guilin _____   admission ticket _____
travel agency _____   fish porridge _____

（3）为画线的词语选择合适的翻译

<u>arrive in</u> Guilin（到了、到达、抵达）
<u>a cruise</u> along the Li River to the town of Yangshuo（乘船、坐船、船游）
<u>magical</u> landscape（好奇的、奇怪的、神奇的）
<u>Chinese</u> lunch（中国、中式、中国人）
no <u>food or drinks</u> from outside（吃的东西和喝的东西、吃的和喝的、食物和饮料）

3. 语体色彩和感情色彩

（1）语体色彩的对应

语体色彩是语言在不同的使用环境中所表现出的一些差别；比如同样的内容，口头上说和把它写下来，或者在不同的场合说和写，所用的词语、句子、语气等会有所不同。语体色彩最常见的表现是口语和书面语的差别。下面是电影《联排（复式）公寓》（*Duplex*）的一段独白（口语语体），画线的词语和句子有较强的口语色彩，括号里是倾向于用在书面语中的词语和句子：

电影独白	翻译	口语色彩
So, you're finally settling down. You've saved up a little nest egg and are ready to dive into the real estate market. Let's do a little shopping around.	这么说,你总算(终于)安顿下来了;也积攒了些钱(有了些积蓄),准备买房子了。	强调直接、形象
The American dream home, ... It's cozy, safe, and just barely within your overstretched budget.	这房子舒适、安全,(而)你紧巴巴(紧张)的预算也刚刚(勉强)可以承受。	简省、形象、直接
... Cozy and affordable, this lovely fixer-upper is the perfect place for a dynamic couple like you...	又舒服又供得起(舒适且负担得起)再好不过了(是最完美的了)	强调、形象
... Well, just a stone's throw away, there is a place with wide-open spaces ...	就几步路远(就在不远处)	形象、夸张
It's almost too good to be true.	天底下有这样的好事吗?(简直难以置信!)	形象、夸张

从上面的例子可以看出,口语色彩的特点是直接、具体、形象、简短,有强调/夸张意味;书面语色彩的特点是比较理性,强调准确、完整和典雅。

与口语和书面语差别有关的,还有表达的正式和非正式之别。在正式场合说话,可以使用一些书面表达,在非正式场合说话,应尽量使用口语的表达。下面是一些"非正式/一般"与"正式"表达的例子:

	一般/非正式	比较正式
breakfast/ lunch/ dinner	早饭/中饭/晚饭	早餐/中餐/晚餐
Mao jackets	毛式夹克	毛式服装
menswear label	男服牌子	男装品牌
casual wear	休闲服	休闲装
read	读的东西	读物
women's magazine	女人的杂志	妇女杂志/女性杂志
ex-boyfriend	以前的男友	前男友
hometown	老家	故乡
buy	买	购买
live	住	居住
begin	开始	着手

续表

	一般/非正式	比较正式
When Candace Shapiro learns that her ex-boyfriend writes an advice column...	知道 写	得知 撰写
then go to Longsheng	然后去龙胜	然后前往龙胜
stay in Para-Para Hotel	住进……	入住
born in 1961	出生在1961年	生于1961年
carries us landscape through this magical landscape	穿过	领略

练习：

翻译中准确表达语体色彩，首先要考虑与原文的对应，即与原文的语体色彩保持一致。请根据下面句子出现的场合，在括号里选择合适的词语或句子。

① Behave, don't piss me off!
　→放规矩点儿，别把我_____了！（激怒，惹毛）

② Check out my new mobile phone. Isn't it cool?
　→瞧我新买的手机，_____吧？（出色，酷）

③ You got to find yourself a rich husband.
　→你须寻觅一位_____。（有钱的老公，富有的夫君）

④ I wonder if you are available this Sunday.
　→_____？
　（不知道这个星期天你是否有空，不知本周日你是否有闲暇）

⑤ My mother's taste never falters.
　→我母亲是个_____的人。（有品位，有鉴赏力）

⑥ Certainly I don't teach because teaching comes naturally to me.
　→我_____教书，_____不是因为生来就是教书的料。（之所以，干；肯定，自然）

⑦ The collapse of copper prices has come just as demand for it from the industrialized world has dropped 8% last year and as production, after two years of high prices, is starting to increase.
　→铜价_____恰好在工业化国家对铜的_____较去年下降8%_____经过两年高价铜的产量开始上升时发生的。（一塌糊涂，暴跌；需求，渴望；跟，且）

131

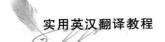

⑧ KEEP DRY AND STAY AWAY FROM HEAT

→ _____ 干燥，_____ 受热（要，保持；不要，切勿）

⑨ Good to the last drop.

→ _____ 香浓，_____。（每一滴，滴滴；还要再喝，意犹未尽）

（2）感情色彩的对应

感情色彩是指词语表现出来的喜爱、憎恶等情感倾向。根据不同的感情色彩，可以把词语分为褒义词（有喜爱义）、贬义词（有憎恶义）和中性词（没有明显的喜爱或憎恶义）。例如：statesman（政治家，褒义）、politician（政客，贬义），praise（赞美，褒义）、flattery（奉承，贬义），hobby（爱好、嗜好，中性）、foible（癖好，贬义），humble（谦逊的，褒义；卑贱的，贬义），aggressive（进取的，褒义；好斗的，贬义）。

练习：

有时词语感情色彩要根据句子使用的环境、表达的目的来判断，翻译时尤应注意选择合适的词语。请判断下面的句子里应使用哪一个词语：

① He (Simpson) also watched with envy and fascination as Mays signed autographs for his fans.（妒忌，羡慕）

② By 1992, he was losing his proudest possession, his wife.（最自豪的，最傲慢的）

③ The coastline has had to be withdrawn as more land is lost to the sea as a result of heavier monsoons and rising sea levels.（结果，后果）

④ He took those cheap flatteries as compliments.（赞美，奉承）

⑤ Don't be shy.（害臊，害羞）

⑥ It is hardly believable that he is as bold as brass.（勇敢，无耻）

⑦ Don't show it around, it just is a cellphone.（显摆，表现）

⑧ The diet imposes overall calorie limits, but daily menus are arbitrary.（武断，随意）

⑨ This young slender lady turned out to be an aggressive executive.（好斗的，有进取心的）

4. 指出并改正译句中的错误

① Cover Girl
→《封面女孩》

② The house is up for sale.
→此房准备卖。

③ The police tried in vain to break up the protest crowds.
→警察尽力驱散人群，但是白费力气。

④ Both parents are careful not to impose their own interests on their children.
→父母亲都很注意不把自己的兴趣放在孩子身上。

⑤ Candidate must be proactive, hard working and have good Microsoft office skills.
→申请者得积极主动、努力工作和好的操作微软办公软件的技巧。

⑥ To do it, she had to swallow her pride.
→为了这样做，她不得不放下她的骄傲。

⑦ Few people knew that he was a hard partyer.
→很少有人知道他热爱社交。

⑧ Financial wealth and ambition were only slightly less favoured.
→良好的经济状况和野心几乎同样受到欢迎。

⑨ USC also had strong connection to Hollywood.
→南加州大学也跟好莱坞有坚强的关系。

⑩ Some interesting diversity came to light.
→一些有趣的差异暴露出来。

⑪ He was not invited to the celebratory dinner.
→他没有被邀请参加庆祝晚饭。

⑫ Search crews worked frantically to rescue him.
→搜救人员疯狂地营救他。

⑬ Sometimes you need to lay back and smell the roses.
→有时你需要放松一下,闻一闻玫瑰花。

⑭ ... human problems, such as diets, loathing of Mondays, apathy ...
→……人类的问题,比如节食、星期一的厌恶、无感情等……

5. 讨论

(1) 说说在时间、金钱等条件都允许的情况下,你最想去的地方。
(2) 有人认为饮食可以体现文化,你是怎么看待饮食和文化的关系的?

补充材料(Supplementary Materials)

Breakfast Menu

Full Breakfast €7.50
4 sausages, 2 rashers, 2 eggs, black & white pudding, hash browns, beans, tea or coffee, toast & brown bread.

Mini Breakfast €5.50
2 sausages, 2 rashers, 1 egg, black & white pudding, tea or coffee, toast & brown bread.

scrambled eggs (4 eggs) €5.00

问题：
① 这是哪种风格的早餐？

② 你早餐一般吃什么？

翻译：
请你翻译这个早餐菜单，注意量词的使用：
_____
_____
_____
_____

Unforgettable Beach Read

Good in Bed by Jennifer Weiner.
This first novel from super-popular Jennifer Weiner is perhaps the funniest and most poignant of them all. When Candace Shapiro learns that her exboyfriend writes an advice column called "Good in Bed" for a new women's magazine,

she is mortified. Cannie's trials and tribulations—weight troubles, men troubles, job troubles—will ring all too true. Don't miss this talented author's debut novel—it'll have you laughing out loud between reaching for your hankie.

(From *Reader's Digest*, Jul. 6, 2005)

问题：

① 被推荐的小说有什么特点？

② 你了解小说的作者吗？

翻译：

① This is perhaps the funniest and most poignant of them all.

② Her trials and tribulations—weight troubles, men troubles, job troubles—will ring all too true.

③ It'll have you laughing out loud between reaching for your hankie.

Outstanding Rocker in China: Cui Jian

Born in 1961, Cui Jian became smitten by Western rock and roll in his early 20s. He has vigorous creativity and passion, continuously a attempting fresh styles. From punk, jazz, and African music to rap, all can be found in his songs, adding to the special Cui-style appeal and power. In 2002, Cui Jian organized and played at the Snow Mountain Music Festival in Lijiang, Yunnan—dubbed the "Chinese Woodstock." The event has been the highest altitude music festival in the world. In the last part of the year Cui Jian launched his "Anti-Lip Synching Movement"—a series of music seminars at universities and other venues throughout China aimed at raising public awareness about the insidious prac-tice of lip synching pervading China's media.

(From Li Li, *Beijing Review*, Dec. 21, 2006)

问题：

① 崔健的歌有什么特点？

② 崔健最近几年开展了什么活动？

翻译：

① born in 1961

② From punk, jazz, and African music to rap, all can be found in his songs.

③ Cui Jian organized and played at the Snow Mountain Music Festival in Lijiang, Yunnan.

Chinese label on show in New York

The image of Chinese fashion, still in the west associated with cheongsam dresses and Mao jackets, has been brought up to date by a catwalk show in New York. The show by Cabbeen, a hugely successful menswear label in China, which now plans to go global, marked the first time a designer from mainland China had taken part in New York fashion week.

The collection, by the 35-year-old designer Cabbeen, featured faded jeans, "vintage" look T-

shirts, customised blazers and designer trainers—all key elements of popular contemporary men's casual wear in New York, Milan and London as well as in Cabbeen's native Guangzhou.

(From Jess Cartner-Morley, *New York*, Feb. 5, 2007)

问题:

你对中国时装的印象如何？

翻译:

The collection, by the 35-year-old designer Cabbeen, featured faded jeans, "vintage" look T-shirts, customised blazers and designer trainers—all key elements of popular contemporary men's casual wear in New York, Milan and London as well as in Cabbeen's native Guangzhou.

Bar in Beijing

Beijing is as busy and vibrant by night as it is by day. From traditional Beijing Opera to flashy discos, from hole-the-wall watering holes to elegant bars, from teahouses to punk rock clubs, whatever your tastes you're sure to find someplace appealing in Beijing.

The capital's drinking scene is a constant work in progress, but Sanlitun Bar Street is where it all started, and it still draws more Friday night expat fun seekers than any other district in Beijing. From hardy perennials like The Tree to tender new shoots like China Doll, there's always something to keep you interested around SLT. Not far away is the Workers' Stadium area ("Gongti"), where Face, Vics and Babyface are three favorites. A more well-heeled crowd chooses CBD venues like Centro, Lan or Aria. The lake area around Hou Hai, deserted just a few short years ago, now rivals Sanlitun for the number and variety of its watering-holes, and offers considerably more scenic appeal.

Try the East Shore Live Jazz Club, La Baie des Anges or—a pioneer in the area and still one of Beijing's most picturesque bars—No Name. Out in the northwest, the Wudaokou/Haidian area with its student ambience has less flash and dash, but offers some of the best entertainment around. Lush is fun day and night, and D-22 is one of Beijing's best live music bars. (Other contenders in that category are Yugong Yishan, Mao Livehouse and the Stone Boat.)

问题：
① 根据短文,北京的酒吧有哪些特色？

② 你愿意去什么样的酒吧？

翻译：
① whatever your tastes you're sure to find someplace appealing.

② the Wudaokou area with its student ambience has less flash and dash, but offers some of the best entertainment around.

Words for the Wise

- Truth will come to light sooner or later.
- Great minds think alike.
- Haste does not bring success.
- Money makes the mare go. (Money talks)
- Sit on the fence
- Love me, love my dog.
- When in Rome, do as the Romans do.
- Paint the lily
- Six of one and half a dozen of the other
- Come straight to the point
- A good gain takes long pain

问题:
请你把这些话翻译成汉语,并比较一下,看看汉语和英语的表达有何异同?

附 录 Appendix

附录1:部分课后练习参考答案
Appendix I: Keys to Some Parts of Main Text Exercises

第一课

2. 词语翻译练习

experience(n.)经验/experience(v.)经历　benefit(n.)好处/benefit(v.)受益
plan(n.)计划/plan(v.)计划　age(n.)年龄/age(v.)衰老
invention 发明/invent 发明　enjoyment 乐趣/enjoy 享受
creativity 创造性/create 创造　strength 力量/strengthen 加强

3. 翻译方法(分译练习)

(2) ① 它得出的结论是:在各种原因中,最主要的是人们从学习外语中所获得的个人益处和乐趣。

② 这700种学习外语的原因被分成70种不同的关键领域,在这些领域里,外语具有显著的作用。

③ 你会学到很多东西,这些东西是你用别的方法学不到的。

④ 他坚持要买另一处房子,其实这房子对他毫无用处。

4. 语法练习

(2) ① 每个人都能从外语学习中受益。

② 学习一种外语的确可以扩大你对不同文化的认识。

③ 多语人群比单一语言人群的思想更加灵活多样。

5. 指出并改正译句中的错误

① 外语扩大你的职业选择

② 每个领域由一个关键词代表

③ 自信地跟自己社区以外的人们互动

④ 如果你正在申请工作,培养交流能力就很重要。

6. 把下面的儿歌翻译成汉语

这就是那只吃了放在杰克盖的屋子里的麦芽糖的老鼠。

第二课

2．词语翻译练习

　　awareness 意识、认识/aware 知道、认识　poison 毒/poisonous 有毒的
　　competence 能力/competitive 有竞争力的　technic 技术/technical 技术上的
　　mechanic 机械师/mechanical 机械的　culture 文化/cultural 文化的

3．翻译方法（倒译练习）

(2)　① 中国的遗产
　　　② 基督纪元的前 14 个世纪
　　　③ 古代和中世纪的中国工匠
　　　④ 它们来自哪里
　　　⑤ 虽然他们是能说会道的理论家
　　　⑥ 技术上的发明肯定比科技思想传播得更快、更远。

4．语法练习

(2)　① 比起亚历山大时代的机械师来，世界更应该感谢古代和中世纪较为沉默的中国工匠。
　　　② 使得中国的科学和技术比起欧洲来在研究价值和令人钦佩的程度上毫不逊色。

5．指出并改正译句中的错误

　　　① （那些影响）在整个 18 世纪持续
　　　② 直接有助于实现基督徒的突破
　　　③ 后来融合到现代科学
　　　④ 西方人接受了却不知道它们来自哪里

第三课

2．词语翻译练习

　　creativity 创造性/flexibility 灵活性/industrialization 工业化/concretization 具体化/broaden 加宽、拓宽/strengthen 加强/mislead 误导/misunderstand 误解/possible 可能的/plausible 可行的/partnership 合作（关系）/friendship 友谊/profit-making 赢利性的/Oscar-winning 获得奥斯卡奖的

3．翻译方法（增译练习）

(2)　①（阿帕亚负责）两家餐馆和 140 名员工。
　　　② 卡西·舒尔曼说表现是最重要的。
　　　③ 使你自己表现出良好的状态和快乐的情绪。

④ 我们没有高尔夫,所以我们建立其他形式的支持团队。
⑤ 保护大脑,使其免受衰老的影响。
⑥ 他是一个有德行的哲学家,而非宗教信仰的传教士。
⑦ (但是除了这些之外,对于文艺复兴时期的早期现代科学也有重要影响)并在整个十八世纪持续。

4. 语法练习
(2) ① 犯错误并不要紧。
② 学习一门外语的词汇要花那么长时间。
③ 猜测一个陌生词语的意思通常是不可能的。
④ 外面有很多反对者。
⑤ 减肥是没有免费的午餐的。
⑥ 那个计划有些创造性。

5. 指出并改正译句中的错误
① 要想在商业上取得成功,你必须想赢。
② 对你的决定有信心。
③ 坐汽车去那儿比骑自行车还慢。
④ 在男性和女性中间都有喜欢兼职工作的。
⑤ 别让那些事情困扰你。

第四课

2. 词语翻译练习
keyword 关键词(短语) / interact 互动(词) / otherwise 否则的话(短语) / overcome 克服(词) / nationwide 全国范围的(短语) / download 下载(词) / mailbox 邮箱(词) / underrate 低估(词) / waistline 腰围(词) / ballroom 舞厅(词) / byproduct 副产品/副作用(词)

3. 翻译方法(转译练习)
(2) ① 女性觉得她们必须表现得很友善。
② 虽然天气不好,他们还是决定去。
③ 阿帕亚负责两家餐馆。
④ 外面有很多人反对。
⑤ 这相当于行走一英里。
⑥ 活力增加了,压力减小了。
⑦ 要保持减肥每天可能至少需要运动60到90分钟。

4. 语法练习

(2) ① (30分钟中等强度的活动可以)把210大卡左右的热量消耗掉。
② 在英国,64％的人把他们的朋友看作是主要的支持者。
③ (有人破坏的话)我就把他们像癌一样切掉
④ 别把要钱看作是不优雅或者低贱的事情
⑤ (如果她桌上有什么事情看起来难办)她就首先处理这件事
⑥ 把耐力训练的时间安排进你忙碌的工作周里去。

5. 指出并改正译句中的错误
① 我把钥匙忘在车里了
② (在一阵突然的狂怒中)他开枪把他们中的一个杀死了
③ 一个新的习惯形成
④ 你在正确的道路上
⑤ 他在工作中出了事故
⑥ 每个新词都要一个一个地学会

第五课

2. 词语翻译练习

(pop)star 明星(偏正) / marriage 婚姻(并列) / remind 提醒(偏正) / regret 后悔(偏正) /kidnap 绑架(并列) / ban 禁止(并列) / young 年轻(主谓) / scream 尖叫(偏正) / dream 梦想(偏正) / witness 目击(主谓)

3. 翻译方法(省译练习)

(2) ① 被判绑架罪
② 我无法同意你的话。
③ 每个人都往前挤。
④ 他遇到后来成为他终身战友的奥利弗·坦博。
⑤ 民主梦想激励着他
⑥ 可以翻译成更加具体、更有区别性的"兄弟和姐妹",或者更加抽象、笼统的"同胞"。

4. 语法练习

(2) ① (最新的研究显示)化学成分,即所谓的烷基胺
② 虽然它们的作用尚未经科学证实
③ 700个理由被分成70个关键领域。
④ 每分钟80步算是慢步伐
⑤ 翻译的意思由情境和语境决定,而不是由词典决定。

⑥ 茶可能是消费最广泛的饮料。
(4) ①（√） ②（×） ③（×） ④（×） ⑤（√）
5. 指出并改正译句中的错误
① 女性倾向于等待机会的到来并抓住它。
② 我们在谈论我的未来。
③ 曼德拉当选为总统。
④ 一个武装盗贼
⑤ 在卢旺达有一支由奥利佛上校领导的联合国部队。
⑥ 每年有 382,000 多人因皮肤癌而接受治疗。
⑦ 每天至少需要 60 到 90 分钟才能维持减肥。
⑧ 当他登上讲台时，人群的叫喊声震耳欲聋。

第六课

2. 词语翻译练习

divorce 离婚(动宾) / group(v) 分组(动宾) / promote 促进(补充) / innovate 创新(动宾) / adventure 冒险(动宾) / become 变成(补充) / define 定义(动宾) / succeed 成功(动宾) / grandfather 爷爷(重叠) / lie(v) 说谎(动宾)

3. 翻译方法（复译练习）

① 普遍存在于茶，还有红酒、苹果、蘑菇以及其他一些东西里。
② 他是位崇高的哲学家，而不是有着宗教信仰的传教士。
③ 先进的 SIA 仪帮助医生把恶性肿瘤与良性肿瘤区别开来。
④ 这些发现和发明常常被西方接受，却不知道它们来自何处。
⑤ 如果你看到了好处——大多数人也看到了好处……

4. 语法练习

(2a) ① 他内心最深处的悲伤
② 60 分钟中等强度的身体活动
③ 西方对中国最常见的称呼
④ "中国遗产"的三个不同价值
⑤ 从我们家到学校之间七个又长又陡的街区
⑥ 当选为总统的最年长的领导者
⑦ 一个压抑而疯狂的儿童杀手
⑧ 人们亲身从学习外语中得到的好处
⑨ 一种冷麦片粥和水果组成的传统南非早餐

(2b) ⑩ 一座空礼堂里的小椅子

⑪ 帮助你找到适合自己的时间与活动搭配计划

⑫ 身体运动的副产品——更多的活力、减少的压抑感、更好的感觉和更优的睡眠。

5. 指出并改正译句中的错误

① 学习外语的700个理由

② 传到欧洲的技术发明

③ 关于妇女社会角色的最新调查

④ 从这个比较得出的一个惊人结论

⑤ 你对不同文化的认识

⑥ 把耐力训练时间安排进你忙碌的一周里的决心

⑦ 两分钟的步行——比如说,步行到信箱

⑧ 适应一个新的健康习惯,或者丢掉一个不健康的习惯

⑨ 他随着脚后跟摇摆,就像一棵棕榈树一样

第七课

2. 词语翻译练习

(1) 婴儿食品/本来就少的备用食品/光滑的岩石/羊毛袜/救援人员/险峻的乡村道路/悬崖峭壁/岁数小一点的孩子/伐倒的树木/一次令人心碎的经历/路上一张白纸上写着的一段话

(2) 用母乳喂孩子/汽油用光了/备用食品越来越少/据估计走了约八英里/她哭了起来/他给朋友打电话时甚至还开了个玩笑。/这家人从感恩节后的星期天就被困住了/他们想走一条近道,可是拐错了弯,结果发现全家人被困在雪地里,迷失了方向。/在莫斯科,我们在旅馆待了十天,除了啤酒和方便面,什么也没吃。

3. 翻译方法

(2) ① 他们打开了车里的暖气,直到汽油用光。

② 九天后,带着救妻儿的希望,父亲詹姆士•金离开去找救援,他答应找不到人就回来。

③ 我又压抑又想家,所以整天哭。

④ 这时大屠杀开始了,如此突然,又是酝酿已久的。

4. 语法练习

① 四个月后,也就是1997年的9月,父母的态度终于松动了。

② 我曾经遭受过种族歧视,我所在的工厂老板不给我工资。

③ 我以前从未演过戏,非常紧张。

④ 她强行把我们从家里带走,穿过七个又长又陡的街区到学校。

5. 指出并改正译句中的错误
   ① 虽然在监狱里得过肺结核,但是现在很健康。
   ② 他曾经在比利时接受培训,现在在首都基加利管理着一家四星级饭店。
   ③ 1915年以后,全家搬到了印度。

第八课

2. 词语翻译练习
   他妻子给他吃蜂蜜三明治/尽力避免争论的羁绊/发达国家感到了威胁/已经被一片一片地拆卸下来,然后装船运到中国组装

3. 翻译方法(反译练习)
(2) ① 他直到昨天才来。
    ② 我不太愿意做这件事。
    ③ 他们一见面就吵架。
    ④ 这支队伍还没赢过一场比赛。
    ⑤ 你只有读了这本书才会了解他。
    ⑥ 如果期望值这么低,婚姻就会更难了,对吧?

4. 语法练习
   ① 詹姆士·金奇回忆起,当他终于想出怎样写一本关于中国的书时,他的妻子在厨房里给他吃蜂蜜三明治,好让他平静下来。
   ② 当被要求说明自从他的书出版以来业已形成的某些社会力量时,他认定中国的中产阶级即将发挥影响。
   ③ 无论是在书里还是谈话里,他都给出了明确的判断,即中国坚定不移的发展必然引起地缘政治的紧张。
   ④ 但如果你是坐在华盛顿,眼看着中国人正成为像苏丹这种地方的最大投资者,支持着美国视为流氓国家的政府,那就会成为很大的问题。

5. 指出并改正译句中的错误
   ① 例如,这本书不是从中国,而是从多特蒙德开始。
   ② 自从1982年作为学生第一次去了中国,中国就让他着迷。
   ③ 这些公司必须到海外去,因为他们在国内无法生存。

第九课

2. 词语翻译练习
   寻找(课程)/大量阅读商业书籍/努力向别人学习/对其他来源作出回应/在

树藤上枯萎 / 运用书上读到的东西 /把自己变成企业家 /产业界也可能提供教育

3. 翻译方法（分译或合译练习）

(2) ① 每当从书上或是参加的讲座中得到新的想法，我就制定一个行动计划来实施它。

② 世界级畅销书《E神话的再次造访》的作者，堪称最优秀的小企业教育家之一的迈克尔·杰伯尔，对引领行业的企业家与凭一技之长在其中工作的人做出了区分。

③ 中国的有些发展被描画成权力的角逐，实际上这是国家薄弱之处的种种表现。

4. 语法练习（复句练习）

(2) ① 我们这个时代一些了不起的企业（如麦当劳）的出现，是因为这些生意人把自己变成了企业家，而不再翻烤肉类饼。

② 故宫里的（星巴克）店自从2000年开业起就引起了争议。虽然去掉了商标牌以保持低调，但是本周这家咖啡店面临着更为激烈的反对。

5. 指出并改正译句中的错误

① 由于过于依赖发明者本人，这种生意常常难以推销（扩大）。

② 他们买很多书，但是他们读书并把书上的东西付诸实践。

③ 最好的书不一定是商业书籍，而常常是自我发展的书，这些书帮助他们成为更好的经理和领导。

④ 制造业在中国是一个残酷的市场，利润很低，这些公司向海外发展是迫不得已，因为它们在国内很难生存。

第十课

2. 词语翻译练习

(1) 总体价值观/面谈/所有可行的方法/全球变暖/工作面试/用于……的（钱应该得到保证）

(2) 五个国家中的四个/三分之二/一半到三分之二的回复者 / 少于10%

(3) 已婚 / 开展 / 第一批 / 随意的 / 雄心 / 良好的 / 显示 / 生儿育女 / 令人吃惊

3. 翻译方法

(2) ① 转译

② 倒译、转译

③ 转译

④ 倒译

⑤ 倒译

⑥ 倒译、省译

⑦ 倒译

4. **语法练习**

(2) ① 人们过去认为男子应该工作而妇女应该照顾家庭。

② "电通"的结论是，日本人变得更加倾向于休闲娱乐，他们看重工作的传统意识已经变弱，尤其是在青年一代中间。

③ 在这个家里是怀特太太做主，而不是她的先生。

④ 他说的都是假话，而我还信以为真。

⑤ 我们相信他，而他也从不让我们失望。

⑥ 这个工程带来的不是繁荣，而是毁坏。

⑦ 萨里很开心，而我却很难堪。

⑧ 这里的天气冬天很冷，而夏天又酷热难当。

⑨ 这双鞋一定很舒服。我敢打赌你可以一整天穿着这双鞋走路而不会觉得累。

⑩ 这所房子十分宽敞，邻居友善，整个住宅区规模不小；而它又是你能承受的。这几乎好得让人难以相信啊。

⑪ 刚到这座城市的时候我才14岁，母亲刚刚自杀了，而继父还在监狱里。

(4) ① 作为一个运动员，她比我更好。

② 这双鞋子更合我脚。

③ 我认为我比别人更了解你。

④ 精神贫乏比物质匮乏更糟糕。

⑤ 这两件衣服你更喜欢哪件？

⑥ 虽然薪水跟过去一样，但是新工作使他有更多的时间待在家里。

⑦ 学习让聪明的更聪明，笨的更笨。

⑧ 最糟糕的是，垃圾商品、有害的促销毁坏人们的品位，扭曲人们对生活的态度。

⑨ 越是对别人知之甚少，越是自视甚高。

⑩ 比起自由竞争的方法，人们更喜欢用市场规范的方法改善生活。

5. **指出并改正译句中的错误**

① 他还未痊愈，不过已经好多了。

② 这双鞋子更合我的脚。

③ 她是一个23岁、刚刚结婚、正准备做一份暑假工作的法律专业学生。

④ 这种愿望在孟买最强，而在日本最弱。
⑤ 像欧盟一样，中国也有实现节能目标的重大需求。
⑥ 我想我比别的人更了解你。
⑦ 读者和一些作家联合请求 J.K. 罗琳不要在第七部，也就是最后一部书中杀死哈利•波特。
⑧ 但是，国内对于中国语言文学所表现的兴趣，比起那两个国家来要小得多。

第十一课

2．词语翻译练习
(1) 网上申请／联系方式／通讯地址／上司、上级／雇员／雇主／领域／截止日期／日程表／附带
(2) 以及、除了……还……／详细地／把……寄到……／对……很熟悉／录取到／全额资助
(3) 出生日期／所获学位／书面／最理想的推荐人／八年以上／顶头上司

3．翻译方法
(2) ① 在妇女对工作的期待方面
② 对于雇主提供托儿服务
③ 对于模拟感染病毒进行的一种防御的强度
④ 与好莱坞联系密切
⑤ 只有他自己才明白的谜
⑥ 对于攻读硕士或更高学位的学生来说
⑦ 批评这部电影突出保罗和上校两个人
⑧ 拿走了商标牌以降低姿态
⑨ 在我最低迷的时候
⑩ 而工作保障名列第二
⑪ 他没有被邀请参加她们的庆祝晚餐
⑫ 羡慕而痴迷地

4．特殊表达的翻译
(1) ① 申请者需英文流利且现居上海或一旦录用能马上迁到上海。
② 申请者应积极主动、努力工作、具备良好的微软办公软件操作技能，能够在上午工作。
(2) ① 五年或五年以上管理工作经验
② 大学或同等学位

③ 高级管理经验或潜能
④ 带厨房的新两居,位于北京市中心

第十二课

2. 词语翻译练习

(1) 食宿/ 观光/ 规定的/ 花费/ 收费/ 保险

(2) 旅游路线/国家公园/返回桂林/门票/旅行社/鱼粥

(3) 到达/ 乘船/ 神奇的/ 中式/ 食物和饮料

3. 语体色彩和感情色彩

(1) ① 惹毛
② 酷
③ 富有的夫君
④ 不知道这个星期天你是否有空
⑤ 有品位
⑥ 之所以;自然
⑦ 暴跌;需求;且
⑧ 保持;切勿
⑨ 滴滴;意犹未尽

(2) ① 羡慕
② 最自豪的
③ 后果
④ 赞美
⑤ 害羞
⑥ 无耻
⑦ 显摆
⑧ 随意
⑨ 有进取心的

4. 指出并改正译句中的错误
① 《封面女郎》
② 此房待售
③ 警察企图驱散抗议人群,但没有成功。
④ 父母亲都很注意不把自己的兴趣强加在孩子身上。
⑤ 申请者需积极主动、努力工作、具备良好的微软办公软件操作技能。
⑥ 为了这样做,她不得不放下架子。

⑦ 很少有人知道他热衷于社交。
⑧ 良好的经济状况和雄心壮志几乎同样受欢迎。
⑨ 南加州大学也跟好莱坞关系密切。
⑩ 表现出来一些有趣的差异。
⑪ 他没有被邀请参加庆祝晚宴。
⑫ 搜救人员奋力营救他。
⑬ 有时你需要放松一下,享受生活。
⑭ 人类的问题,比如节食、星期一综合征、冷漠等。

附录 2：补充材料参考译文及部分练习答案
Appendix II: Sample Translations of the Supplementary Materials and Keys to Some Parts of Supplementary Exercises

第一课

语言的任意性

　　语言中无处不在的任意性是我们耗费大量时间学习一门外语词汇的主要原因。通常我们不可能猜到一个陌生词语的意思，因此我们只能一个一个地学习生词。

　　语言的任意性决定了科幻电影里推崇的"万能翻译机"是不可能的。大家熟悉这样的场景：我们勇敢的太空探险者登上了一个新的星球，碰到讲着完全陌生语言的外星人，然后他们拿出"万能翻译机"拨两下，转眼间那种外族语言就变成了地道的美式英语。还有更为现实一点的情况是，即使你已经知道了几千巴斯克语的词汇，当有人跟你说"小心！别撞到那个 lupu"的时候，你会因为 lupu 对你来说是生词而无从知道它到底是个捕熊的陷阱、一条毒蛇、一个强盗，还是一头饿狼。实际上，它是一只蝎子。所以，语言的任意性决定了"万能翻译机"万能是不可能的。

翻译参考答案：
①—⑥略
⑦ 通常我们不可能猜到一个陌生词语的意思。
⑧ 你无从知道 lupu 到底是个捕熊的陷阱、一条毒蛇、一个强盗，还是一头饿狼。

词语的意义与翻译

　　语言间各组成部分及其意义关联的不同对翻译有两个影响：首先，意义的翻译应该由情境和语境决定，而不应照搬字典。其次，翻译总是或多或少地丢掉或改变一些东西。

　　正如凯特福特（Catford）所说，"源语言和目标语之间从来没有完全的意义对应……"。语言之间意义差异的第二个影响，决定了界定翻译方法的种类——以避免不恰当的对译成为翻译理论的一个任务。

　　具体化——翻译中上下位关系的转换使翻译内容具体化或者区别化，例如，

153

德语Geschwister可以翻译成更具体而又有区别性的brothors and sisters("哥哥/弟弟"和"姐姐/妹妹"),或者翻译成更概括、不加区分的一个词siblings(兄弟/姐妹),这取决于语境和翻译的要求。

逻辑推导——英语中"更短的工作时间(shorter working hours)"表示行为的结果,而德语和法语中的对应词Senkung der Aebeitszeit和reduction de la semaine de travail表示的却是一个行为的原因。

反译法——是一种常用的从相反的角度翻译的方法,可以翻译出在目标语中听起来更自然的说法。因此法语est une valeur déjà ancienne可以从字面上译成"是一种过时的价值",但是也可以翻译成"绝对不是一种新的价值"。

补偿法——是在翻译一种仅限于源语言存在的东西时用到的翻译方法。在电影《人咬狗》当中,一个连环杀手正和朋友们用餐,突然一阵无名火让他射杀了其中的一个朋友;在这儿一位译者谨慎地将常用的tu改为更显尊敬的vous,这是对缺少一个完全对应的词的弥补,因为翻译成"Sir"也是个常用但不尽恰当的办法。

问题参考答案:
① 略。
② 具体化、逻辑推导、反译法、补偿法。
③ concretization:把德语Geschwister翻译成"哥哥/弟弟"和"姐姐/妹妹"。
　logical derivation:英语中shorter working hours在译为德语或法语时要注意是表原因还是表结果。
　antonymic translation:法语est une valeur déjà ancienne翻译成"绝对不是一个新的价值"。
　compensation:在翻译法语时直接引入法语词vous。

第二课

西方语言里的"中国"

西方语言对中国的称呼最常见的大概是Seres,Sina和Cathay。Seres这一名称来源于中国的丝绸,希腊人将其传到欧洲并称之为"ser"。Seres作为中国之称显然和大约始于公元前220年的丝绸贸易有关。Sina是拉丁文,China一词正是从Sina而来,但Sina这个称呼可能并不是源于罗马,而是在公元前2世纪的时候来自印度:由梵文称呼古代中国"秦"的一个词转化而来。

"秦"之后的朝代更迭使中国又有了其他各种称呼,公元10世纪辽代的部落名称"契丹",被翻译成俄文Khitai,进而形成欧洲语言用Cathay来称呼同一个国家——中国;正如古代的Sina和Seres不过对于这两组称呼的演变关系,都已有人提出质疑,因为它们可能一个来自陆地传播,而另一个来自海上传播。

问题参考答案:
① 可能来自罗马,但也可能来自梵文对古代中国"秦"的称呼。
② 中西方联系和传播的途径不同以及朝代更迭。

翻译参考答案:
① 西方语言对于中国的称呼最为世人所知的是 Seres、Sina 和 Cathay。
② Seres 作为中国之称显然和大约始于公元前 220 年的丝绸贸易有关。

孔 子

我们根据什么标准把孔子而不是释迦牟尼或基督列入十大思想家?——仅仅一个原因就足够了:他是位崇高的哲学家而不是宗教信仰的传道者;他基于现世行动而倡导崇高,而不是基于超自然的信奉;他更像苏格拉底而不是像耶稣。

生于(公元前 552 年)礼崩乐坏、诸侯纷争的时代,孔子致力于恢复礼乐、匡正天下。如何实现呢?孔子认为:古之圣贤,欲明明德于者必先治其国,欲治其国者必先齐其家,欲齐其家者必先修其身,欲修其身者必先正其心,诚其意,欲正心诚意者必先格物至知。这些思想中都包含了明确的道德和政治哲学。

一个学生曾问孔子是否该以德报怨,孔子回答:"如果那样你将如何报德?以德报德,至于恶呢,应当用正义来对待它。"此外,他不认为人人生而平等,也不认为每个人都有同样的智力。

鲁国名城"中都"采纳了孔子的主张并任命孔子为中都宰,据说,"民风大治,犯罪、欺诈、不敬等行为销声匿迹"。……孔子逝后,他的弟子们在他的坟前修庐守陵,像对父亲一样,守了将近三年。其中最敬爱孔子的子贡在别的弟子离去后,又独自守了三年。

问题参考答案:
① 他是位崇高的哲学家而不是宗教信仰的传道者;他基于现世行动而倡导崇高,而不是基于超自然的信奉;他更像苏格拉底而不是更像耶稣。
② 恢复礼乐、匡正天下。

翻译参考答案:
① 孔子去世后
② 犯罪行为销声匿迹
③ 他不认为每个人都有同样的智力。
④ 名城"中都"采纳了孔子的主张并任命孔子为中都宰。

第三课

欧洲女性角色的变化

近期对女性社会角色的调查显示,即使在西欧这样的工业化国家之间也存在文化的多样性。在一项欧洲跨国研究中,年龄在 18 到 65 岁的女性被问到"通常在女性的生活中,哪个群体的人给予她们各方面最大的支持?",回馈中分别有 71% 和 80% 的人提到了"她们的家庭"。在英国,64% 的人还提到了"她们的朋友",而在意大利和西班牙这项数据分别只占 23% 和 17%。

在对比中可得出的一个显著结论是,英国和意大利的女性和男性对于部分时间工作(或兼职工作)意愿相同,而在其他国家,尤其是德国,数据虽并不一致,但是相近。仅仅在欧洲的范围内,这项调查就显示了女性想要从工作中获得的东西不同。在英国,灵活的工作时间最为女性看重,位列第二的是工作稳定,而只有不到三分之一的人会看重工作的刺激性和挑战性。但是,在意大利,关注工作是否有意思的人占到 51%,在法国也达到 44%。在西班牙,工作是否稳定是考虑一份工作的最重要的方面。英国女性还比较优先考虑雇方在托儿服务方面的条款。

问题参考答案:
① 灵活的工作时间。
② 因文化差异而具体情况不同。

翻译参考答案:
① 年龄在 18 到 65 岁的妇女
② 非常重视雇主是否提供托儿服务
③ "她们的家庭"被看作是最能提供支持的

性别之战:男人和女人撒不同的谎吗?

男性和女性谁更诚实一点?虽然我们的调查显示男性和女性在撒谎方面有不同的表现,不过他们似乎都不是无辜的。

男性不诚实的行为更多地表现在非个人事务上。他们比女性更可能盗窃公共财产(71% 男性比 61% 女性),骗得退税(24% 比 15%),非法下载音乐(43% 比 35%)。

美国新泽西州罗伯特伍德约翰逊医学院的心理学家迈克尔·刘易斯说:"男性更愿意冒险。"他们会谋划实施不诚实的行为,而女性则倾向于等待机会到来时抓住它。此外,刘易斯说,"女性在人际方面撒谎更多一些"。虽然这些行为在两性当中都会出现,但其中存在明显的性别倾向。

工作当中,女性盗窃公共财物的频率不像男性频繁,但她们会比男性更多地用撒谎请病假(64%的女性比58%的男性)。生活当中,女性会通过撒谎避免矛盾,例如谎报近期购买的一个东西的花费(34%比25%),或者为照顾他人的感受而违心地说"这条裤子一点都不让你的臀部显得肥。"(74%比65%)。

问题参考答案：
① 盗窃公共财产,骗得退税等。
② 撒谎请病假,谎报近期购买的一个东西的花费等。

翻译参考答案：
① 男性更愿意冒险
② 女性盗窃公共财产的频率不像男性频繁
③ 女性倾向于等待一个机会来临再加以利用

第四课

茶有助于提高免疫力和皮肤保健

除水之外,茶可能是世界上日常消费最多的饮料。现在,新的研究不断提供的越来越多的证据表明,茶不仅是一种受欢迎的饮品,而且对身体有诸多好处。一个新的研究显示了茶中发现的物质是怎样帮助人体免疫系统抵制感染的。另一个报告也指出绿茶中的成分可能有助于皮肤细胞的再生。

这项最近的研究显示,茶(还有酒、苹果、蘑菇等)中含有的一种叫作烷基胺的化学物质也存在于一些细菌、真菌、癌细胞、寄生虫以及其他致病寄体中。研究者波士顿哈佛医学院的免疫学家杰克·布考斯基说,饮茶可以使抗病免疫细胞识别并记住烷基胺,从而提高免疫系统抵抗这些寄体的能力。布考斯基的团队做了一个实验,让血细胞在试管中接触这些烷基胺化学物质,能够使血细胞抵抗模拟感染的效果增强五倍。相反,没有接触过烷基胺的血细胞对模拟的细菌感染没有明显的反应。

斯蒂芬·苏是佐治亚州医学院的一位茶保健研究者和细胞生物学家,他在《制药学和实验疗法》杂志上发表的研究成果显示:茶中的一些化学物质可以激活老化的皮肤细胞。斯蒂芬·苏说这项发现或许将来不仅可以用于研制抗衰老药品,也可以用于治疗伤口愈合和改善皮肤状况,一些抗衰老的化妆品已经采用了茶中的提取物,虽然它们的作用还没有经过科学证明。

问题参考答案：
① 茶(还有酒、苹果、蘑菇等)中含有的一种叫作烷基胺的化学物质也存在于一些细菌、真菌、癌细胞、寄生虫以及其他致病寄体中。饮茶可以使抗病免疫细胞识别并记住烷基胺,从而提高免疫系统抵抗这些寄体的能力。
② 茶里的一些化学物质可以激活老化的皮肤细胞。

翻译参考答案：
① 让血细胞在试管中接触这些（烷基胺）化学物质
② 使抵抗模拟感染的效果增强五倍
③ 这项发现将来或许不仅可以用于研制抗衰老药物，也可以用于治疗伤口愈合和改善皮肤状况。

新癌症扫描仪——日光爱好者的救星

澳大利亚每年新诊断出的癌症病例中皮肤癌患者占到81％。每年超过382,000人接受皮肤癌治疗，1,300多人会失去生命。现在，一种能够在早期发现癌细胞的简易扫描仪能够挽救人们的生命，使众多澳大利亚人免于死于皮肤癌。

这项先进的扫描技术可以测量黑色素、胶原蛋白乃至皮下两毫米的受损组织的颜色，因此医生可以据此区分致命的痣和良性的痣。悉尼医师克瑞·费尔普斯说"预防和尽早检测出皮肤癌细胞都非常重要，如果这项技术意味着医生们可以较早地发现癌细胞，那么也就意味着我们谈的是挽救生命的技术。"

来自诺斯邦迪（位于悉尼东部）的28岁的彼特·罗根把这项检测称为"真相检查"。罗根女士说她在检测过自己的痣后，虽然医生认为她的痣是良性的，但她还是很注意自己在阳光下待的时间，作为自己珍爱生命行动的一部分。她说"这次检测让自己心里有了底，我觉得我应该定期检查一下。虽然我遮盖着并且涂上高防晒指数的防晒霜，但这些并不总是够用。"

虽然这项技术有潜在的挽救生命的作用，但费尔普斯博士（澳大利亚70名使用了这种扫描仪的医生之一）提醒大家，预防皮肤癌的基本准则还是无法替代的。

问题参考答案：
能够在早期发现癌细胞。

翻译参考答案：
① 每年超过382,000人接受皮肤癌治疗。
② 预防和尽早检测出皮肤癌细胞都非常重要。

第五课

《卢旺达饭店》

1994年，一场胡图族人对成千上万图西族人的大屠杀发生在卢旺达。保罗·卢斯赛伯吉纳是胡图族人，他娶了一位图西族妻子——坦缇安娜。他曾经在比利时接受培训，现在在卢旺达首都基加利经营着一家叫米勒科林斯的四星级饭店。他经营得非常好。他知道如果有长官的公文包寄存在饭店，那么取回时要在里面放上几瓶苏格兰威士忌。他知道要想进口他想要的啤酒,行贿是必需的。他知道他的顾客习惯于奢侈,即使在这样一个夹在坦桑尼亚、乌干达和刚果之间的中非小国也应提供他们所要的奢华。因为他的这些"知识",就能说他是一个坏人吗?恰恰相反。这些知识让他成为一个识时务的行家。因为他的这些"知识",他的饭店才运营良好,大家也才能皆大欢喜。

但是,突然之间,种族灭绝开始了,经营多年的卢旺达饭店开始遭遇麻烦。非洲问题迭起是因为欧洲殖民势力在非洲建立国家政权的时候对非洲本来的部族隔阂视而不见,相互敌视的部落也被赶到同一块土地上。比利时对卢旺达多年的殖民统治中,图西族统治并杀害了不少胡图族人。

现在胡图族人统治卢旺达了,军队在全国各地横行,杀害图西族人。奥利弗上校代表联合国驻在卢旺达,他将自己目睹的一切报告给上级,请求帮助和干预,但是无人理会。保罗·卢斯赛伯吉纳也将不断加剧的灾难反映给在布鲁塞尔的集团总部,但是基加利的这个饭店对整个集团的链条来说并非关注的重点。结果,奥利弗上校和保罗这两个人只好单枪匹马地行动,挽救了上千人的生命。

《卢旺达饭店》2004年在多伦多首映的时候,有些杂志批评它聚焦在保罗和那个上校身上,而没有全面地描绘整个种族灭绝的屠杀。但是导演特里·乔治和编剧科尔·皮尔森无疑做了正确的决定。一部电影不可能描绘成千上万的屠杀者,但能够反映少数一部分人是怎么做的。保罗是个真实的人,奥利弗上校也是基于某个原型,整个《卢旺达饭店》是在真实地反映他们当时是怎么做的。

问题参考答案:
懂得人情世故,知道行贿,知道给他的顾客提供所要的奢华。
翻译参考答案:
① 娶了一位图西族妻子叫坦缇安娜
② 他曾经在比利时接受培训。
③ 有些杂志批评它聚焦在保罗和上校身上,而没有全面描绘整个种族屠杀。

我的父亲甘地

1948年,印度。当孟买的警察在街头救起一个垂危的乞丐,为了给他登记住院,他们问他父亲的名字时,这个乞丐的回答竟然是莫罕达斯·卡拉姆昌德·甘地!

众所周知,甘地的非暴力思想和他领导的"退出印度"运动使英国承认了印度独立和巴基斯坦建国,但他的家庭生活却鲜为人知。这部传记电影试图弥补这一缺失。电影讲述了被人们称为圣雄或巴布(父亲)的甘地和他四个儿子之中最大的哈里拉尔之间破损的关系。

用闪回的方式,电影描述了甘地一家在南非逗留时的紧张关系,那时甘地担任律师,直到 1915 年。作为一家之长,甘地坚决要求哈里拉尔放弃他的学业和妻子——古拉,辅助自己与不平等的种族隔离制度作斗争。这致使年轻的哈里拉尔心生怨恨。

  1915 年,甘地一家搬回了印度,那里抵抗英帝国的势头正旺。哈里拉尔努力维持自己的独立,却被投机分子利用,他们打着甘地的名义建立了一些没有信用的公司从而败坏了自由运动。甘地公开和他任性的儿子断绝了关系。哈里拉尔于是沉湎于酒精,消沉下去。

  弗洛兹·阿巴斯·汗(导演)的第一部电影是根据他的同名舞台剧改编的,探索一个在现代印度属于禁忌的话题:甘地式理想主义的隐患。确实,这部电影已经在印度掀起了争论。

  没有必要大惊小怪。电影在甘地遗属的协助下完成,弗洛兹·阿巴斯·汗的电影坚定地采取中立立场,把主人公们都塑造成身处个人难以控制的环境下具有缺陷的人。

问题参考答案:
甘地父子关系决裂。
导演不表达立场,而把主人公都塑造成个人不可控制的环境下有缺陷的人。
翻译参考答案:
① 他的非暴力思想为人熟知。
② 他们打着甘地的名义建立了一些没有信用的公司从而败坏了自由运动。

第六课

他们的故事和我的很相似

  当我告诉我妈妈我想去英国工作时,她一下子哭了。我是我们家四个孩子当中最小的,而且身体也不好,整个童年,妈妈都照顾着我。她说:"你路上病了怎么办?"但是我已经给我们当地的蛇头打了电话。虽然蛇头都是人贩子,但是(整个过程)就像给一个旅行社打电话一样简单,只是贵很多:15,000 英镑,我明天就可以走。

  我曾经看过伦敦桥和红色的公共汽车的照片。一个朋友在那儿赚了大钱。四个月以后,1997 年的 9 月,父母让了步。我们就找邻居谈,他是一个我们信得过的蛇头。花 13,000 英镑,他就可以把我弄到英国,这在平均工资只有 30 英镑的津盼(Jinfen)差不多是一处好房子的价钱。家里跟亲戚朋友借了钱,我要为这笔借款付利息。

  我以为我很快就可以还钱,但事实上非常困难。去英国的路上花了六个月。我们是一群人一起走。每到一个国家,我们都会被转给一个新的蛇头,带我们去新的国家。在莫斯科,我们在一个店里住了10天,只有方便面和啤酒。在乌克兰,我们在火车上睡着的时候被警察拘留了,(但后来)他们竟放我们走了。又过了一个月之后,从捷克共和国的一间阴暗的房间里出来,我们被装进了卡车,驶向荷兰。当我们在伦敦利物浦大街下了火车的时候,我知道旅途结束了,只是感到空虚和一无所有。

　　我花了六年的时间还清债务。为了每周150英镑,我每天得工作11个小时。我是那么沮丧并且想家,以至于一直悲泣。我干的什么事?我在津盼经营金银首饰店,现在却比我在中国的朋友工作辛苦得多。

　　在最低谷的时候,我加入了伦敦北部国王十字街的华人基督教会。佩斯特劳伦斯像朋友一样照顾我,并说服我去参演《鬼佬》。这部电影是讲述2004年在莫克姆贝湾丧生的23名拾贝的中国人的生活困境。虽然我没有拾贝,但他们生活的条件和我自己的非常相像:一间房子,打地铺,墙壁的油漆剥落。跟他们一样,我也常遭遇种族虐待,而且有一次工厂的老板拒绝付我工资。

　　我以前从未表演过,所以非常紧张。我还是个单亲妈妈,(因此)感到很羞愧。我有个儿子叫肖恩,现在六岁了,我鼓了很大的勇气才告诉父母我怀孕了,只有很少的人知道我有个孩子。现在我有了一些朋友和支持我的人。我现在在伯明翰的一所学院里每周学三天英语。

　　我父母没有看过这部电影。他们并不以我为荣。他们希望,我也希望,我是在中国。但既然我定居在这里了,我坚信我的未来会好起来。

问题参考答案:

① 征得父母同意,找当蛇头的邻居谈,跟亲朋借钱,然后经由莫斯科、乌克兰、捷克、荷兰到达伦敦。

② 为了每周150英镑,每天得工作11个小时;沮丧并且想家;生活条件很差;常遭遇种族虐待;带一个私生子。

翻译参考答案:

① 我曾经看过伦敦桥和红色的公共汽车的照片。

② 我们就找邻居谈,他是一个我们信得过的蛇头。

③ 花13,000英镑,他可以把我弄到英国,这在平均工资只有30英镑的津盼(Jinfen)差不多是一处好房子的价钱。

第七课

白天和黑夜

　　就在他们的孩子安睡在旁边的时候,他的前妻被割断了喉咙。前妻死后不到12个小时,他作为犯罪嫌疑人被警方传回洛杉矶。不过,当辛普森6月13号早上匆匆赶到芝加哥机场的时候,他还停下来签了一个名。

辛普森案件引起公众巨大关注,以至于很多人能说出那双血迹手套的位置、妮可给她妈妈打电话的时间或者罗纳德·高曼有几处刀捅的伤口。但辛普森自身仍然是一个谜。实际上,他过着双重的生活。作为公司代言人,偶尔和赫兹(全美最大的租车公司)的一些官员喝点啤酒的辛普森还是个聚会迷,有记者发现他出入酒吧、沉迷毒品和女色。

在某种程度上,双重生活是不堪承受的。令人惊奇的是,由下面的故事(我们可以看到),辛普森撑了很久。20世纪50年代,他是"波斯"帮派的一员。他喜欢去袭击当地的馅饼公司,他后来说他最喜欢黑莓馅的。辛普森15岁时因抢劫一家酒类商店在狱中待了一个周末之后,一个社会工作者安排他见了棒球明星威利·梅斯,威利·梅斯说了一番鼓励的话给他,让他战胜困难。后来辛普森说他对梅斯位于城市繁华地带的豪宅更感兴趣。他当时还羡慕而嫉妒地看着梅斯给他的球迷签名。他说:"我想,让人们知道我、喜欢我,愿意像我这样,这感觉多好啊!"

他产生了上大学的念头。虽然成绩不好,但辛普森可以获得几乎任何一个州"橄榄球工厂"的奖学金,不过他选择了南加州大学。这所大学比其他学校有更多的电视上镜率,另外,也因为他们在玫瑰杯比赛中定期出现。南加州大学还和好莱坞有紧密的联系。招收辛普森的助教马文·高克斯同时也是好莱坞的一个演员,他能够帮助辛普森在一个制片厂获得一个做临时演员的暑期工作。

辛普森在戏弄女性方面有严格的双重标准。在1968年的一次采访中,他的前妻玛格丽特说她的丈夫是个"禽兽",他不允许别的年轻的男人和她说话,但是他自己却可以为所欲为……1977年,辛普森遇到了返校节舞会皇后18岁的妮可,当时她在一个迪斯科舞厅做侍女,他们马上就开始了约会。一年以后,辛普森和玛格丽特离了婚,时间大概就是他和妮可开始生活在一起的时候。辛普森和玛格丽特的离婚刚刚办理完,他们襁褓中的女儿艾容就在泳池中溺死了。

到1992年的时候,他开始失去他最引以为荣的所有,即他的妻子。受够了辛普森的虐待和他的拈花惹草,妮可在1992年3月离开了辛普森。虽然辛普森依然玩弄别的女人,但他一直希望妮可回来。6月12日下午,辛普森去一个舞蹈表演会上看他的一个女儿,他没有和妮可说话,也没有被邀请参加他们在曼赞卢那的庆祝晚餐。他钻进他的劳斯莱斯去了麦当劳。接下来的几个小时他干的事将被当作杀人犯审查的结果而公之于世。

据他的一个好朋友称,在案发后的几天中,辛普森好像受了打击并且精神不振,现在他好多了。他在给这个朋友打电话的时候甚至还开了个玩笑。

附 录

问题参考答案：
① 事业成功而个人生活混乱。
② 这所大学比其他学校有更多的电视上镜率，他们在玫瑰杯比赛中定期出现，还和好莱坞有紧密的联系。

翻译参考答案：
① 不到12个小时
② 双重生活会不堪承受
③ 说她的丈夫是个"禽兽"
④ 他被警方传回洛杉矶作为犯罪嫌疑人接受审讯
⑤ 他接下来几个小时干的事将被当作杀人犯审讯的结果公之于世。

第八课

中欧伙伴关系更上一层楼

　　能源保护和气候改变将是未来几年内中欧合作着力加强的核心领域。欧盟委员会有消息称，欧洲将致力于，到2020年主要通过节能措施使温室气体的排放量至少减少20%。另外显示的一个雄心勃勃的目标是，确保欧洲20%的能源供给来自可再生能源。另外，欧盟委员会能源投资的75%将集中在可持续的能源上。欧盟委员会代表团的大使安德烈·阿玻说："同欧盟委员会一样，中国也有达到其节能目标的强烈需求，中国和欧盟现在都在这些领域投放了大量的项目，坚定地突显（这方面的）优先考虑。"欧盟在建筑业、交通业和工业上都拥有高标准、高效能的技术，大使希望能和中国的几个部门合作，例如国家环保总局、国家发改委等，在中国建立一个欧盟清洁能源技术中心。

问题参考答案：
① 能源保护和气候改变。
② 到2020年，主要通过节能措施使温室气体的排放量至少减少20%。另外，确保欧洲20%的能源供给来自可再生能源。

翻译参考答案：
① 中欧合作的核心领域将着力加强。
② 另外一个雄心勃勃的目标是，确保欧洲20%的能源供给来自可再生能源。

网络造势的目标是让星巴克离开紫禁城

　　全球化时代最不协调的景观之一——北京紫禁城的星巴克咖啡店，在一阵激烈的网上宣传活动之后可能很快会成为过去。为了回应这一次网民力量的表现，故宫的监管者们公布了重新考虑星巴克能否存在的计划。

除了肯德基和麦当劳之外,"星巴克",这个来自西雅图的咖啡店,在中国也非常流行。但是位于故宫里面的星巴克店面却从它2000年开业伊始就引发了争论。虽然该店面保持低调,撤掉了有其商标的招牌,但这个店在这一周受到了比以往都强烈的反对。导火索是一个电视节目主持人芮成钢在周一发表的一篇博客,他号召网上宣传抵制这个店面,称其"践踏中国文化"。

星巴克宣称并没有撤离的计划。大中华区副总裁伊登·伍恩对路透社说,"星巴克尊重紫禁城的深厚历史和文化,以一种尊重、与环境相宜的方式运营。""六年多来,我们给成千上万的中外游客提供了一个休息的场所。我们很荣幸能有这个机会……让游客参观博物馆的体验更美好。"

问题参考答案:
① 当地主持人认为这是在"践踏中国文化",而星巴克认为他们尊重了故宫的历史文化,并且为中外游客提供了好的休息场所。
② 略

翻译参考答案:
① 在一阵激烈的网上宣传活动之后可能很快会成为过去。
② 但是位于故宫里面的星巴克店面却从它2000年开业伊始就引发了争论。

第九课

工作压力消耗人

在外企找到一份高薪工作是很多中国求职者梦寐以求的事情,但是最近的一项调查可能改变他们的看法。

根据零点研究资讯集团近来的一项调查,将近90%在外企工作的中国员工忍受着工作病。零点集团说,在1,521个外企员工的反馈中,91%的人报告了各种症状,如筋疲力尽、压力、焦躁、睡眠不足和工作后的肩颈麻木。

采访是在北京、上海、广州和武汉四个城市通过电话、电邮、传真或面对面访谈进行的。据零点集团分析,15.4%接受采访的人说他们忍受着至少七种可能致人崩溃或引起严重疾病的症状。另外有5%的人说他们忍受着至少10种病症,可见他们工作过度。一半的反馈者说他们很少锻炼,同时有很多人抱怨他们每天工作超过10个小时,深夜才回家,周末还要工作。

被采访者最普遍的症状中,30%的人说的是他们记忆力下降、压力大、情绪波动和加速衰老。根据这项调查,中年的高薪员工更容易得工作病。缺乏定期的健康检查,以及诸如抽烟、喝酒、不吃早饭等不良生活方式也会使情况变得更加糟糕。

问题参考答案：
① 工作时间长，工作压力大，没时间锻炼，生活不规律等。
② 记忆力下降，压力大，情绪波动和加快衰老，焦躁，睡眠不足，工作后的肩颈麻木等。

翻译参考答案：
采访是在北京、上海、广州和武汉四个城市通过电话、电邮、传真或面对面访谈进行的。

网络重新定义现实

因特网是按一个键就可以连接上的东西，是一种融入我们的日常生活——以至于很容易会视其为理所当然的东西。但是它的重要和神奇是不管怎么说也不算过分的。专家与我们分享的观点是：因特网由于它的超链接、路由器和光纤电缆等成为现代技术的奇迹。它代表了现代世界的文明。没有任何一个人类历史上的其他发明创造像因特网一样将世界如此联系起来。

我们的专家也同意因特网完全可以称为一个地方，一个人们可以"去"的，可以连接到世界任何其他地方的地方。通过网络摄像机，人们从太空针塔（西雅图的地标建筑）的顶部看西雅图如同观看犀牛和豹子在南非漫步一样地简单。

也许最令人惊奇的是它怎样重新界定"地方"这一概念。例如，在基于网络的、被称为"第二人生"的虚拟世界中，超过百万人已经创造了称作"化身"（avatars）的自己的象征，还建造了一个地方，有现实中原有的景致，有可以在虚拟的商店和活动中流通的货币。

想要一双虚拟的阿迪达斯的鞋子吗？买。想听一场 Duran Duran 乐队的音乐会吗？没有问题。想在一家酒店住宿吗？试试"顷刻成真"酒店吧。诸如此类的让人眩晕的小小妙想每天在头脑中涌现，它们都是将要发生的事情的开端。

问题参考答案：
① 由于它的超链接、路由器和光纤电缆等现代技术，网络将世界联系起来，并融入了我们的生活。
② 略

翻译参考答案：
① 是一种融入我们的日常生活以至我们很容易认为是自然而然的东西。
② 例如，在基于网络的、被称为"第二人生"的虚拟世界中，超过百万人已经创造了称作"化身"（avatars）的自己的象征，还建造了一个地方，有现实中原有的景致，有可以在虚拟的商店和活动中流通的货币。

第十课

《时代周刊》地图集显示全球变暖的影响

一份新的世界地图揭示了全球范围气候变化的严重影响

由于全球变暖,《时代周刊·世界地图集》的制图师不得不重新绘制海岸线、重新划分陆地类型了。自从四年前上一次世界地图集出版以来,有些地方的海平面降低了,有的升高了,同时冰盖缩小了,有的湖接近消失。

该地图的主编米科·阿什沃什说:"我们可以确切地看到环境灾难在我们眼前展开。我们真的担心在不久的将来,一些显著的地理特征会永远消失。"他说最大的罪魁祸首是气候变化和规划糟糕的灌溉工程。一些变化包括:

- 位于中亚的咸海自1967年以来缩小了75%。
- 非洲的乍得湖自1963年以来缩小了95%。
- 死海比50年前降低了25米,相当于5个双层公交的高度。
- 格兰德河、黄河、科罗拉多河以及底格里斯河的部分河段每年夏天都濒临干涸断流。一年中的某些时间里,它们无法流到大海。

由于季风和海平面上涨,很多陆地被淹没在海水中,导致孟加拉国的海岸线后撤。

- 非洲的乞力马扎罗山80%的冰盖在过去的100年中消失了。
- 由于海平面上升,太平洋基里巴斯的岛屿、马绍尔群岛、托克劳群岛、图瓦卢群岛和瓦努阿塔都面临着严重的威胁。

城市化

该地图集称世界人口正日益城市化,在未来的一年中,城市和城镇居民数量将首次超过农村人口数量。

- 1950年以前的一百年中,最大的人口流动发生在欧洲和北美,但在过去的50年中,欠发达国家的城市人口急剧增长。
- 到2030年,五分之三的人口(59.9%)将成为城市人口,全球城市人口预计增长到49亿。1970年的时候是13亿。
- 在2010年到2030年间,世界新的城市人中六分之五的会是非洲人和亚洲人。
- 1950年只有纽约人口超过1,000万,而现在有18个城市达到这个规模。
- 到2015年,达到这一规模的城市预计将有22个,包括非洲的首批"大城市"——拉各斯和开罗。

好消息

- 世界13%的陆地表面现在被覆盖在全球超过107,000个规划保护区域里。
- 2004年到2005年间世界风能增长了20%以上。

- 被萨达姆·侯赛因抽干的伊拉克美索布达米亚湿地的大部分现在正在得到回灌。
- 为阻止咸海北部因海水外流而急剧退缩兴建起来的一座大坝正在使海面回升。渔业正在恢复,饮食质量得到提高,人们身体更加健康了。
- 今年有22个新的景点,包括悉尼歌剧院和科孚旧城,被列入联合国教科文组织的世界文化和自然遗产名录,使该名单上的遗产总数达到了851个。

问题参考答案:
① 气候变化和糟糕的灌溉工程。
② 略

翻译参考答案:
① 在不久的将来
② 在我们眼前展开
③ 我们真的担心……
④ 自从四年前世界地图最后一次出版以来,有些地方的海平面降低了,有的升高了。
⑤ 死海比50年前降低了25米,相当于5个双层公交的高度。
⑥ 为阻止咸海北部因海水外流而急剧退缩兴建起来的一座大坝正在使海面回升。

第十一课

杰普招聘公关管理/销售经理

杰普正为设在上海的财务部门的一个重要职位招聘人员。该岗位人员将学习从寻找潜在客户到协同财务投资组合研究分析委员会制定财务投资组合过程中的一切。

申请者需英语流利且现居上海,或者在获得这个职位后可以马上迁到上海。掌握第二外语者优先考虑。申请者需有销售经验,这将是其基本职责。

财务顾问的职责包括:发展或建立客户资源;促进杰普财务服务的发展;约定潜在客户;组织与客户的会议,根据他们的目标和需要推荐财务产品;对公司业绩的不断增长负有责任;组织小组研讨,参加每月聚餐活动以有效获得客户推荐。

你能得到什么? 福利报酬很有竞争力,将在面试的时候商谈。如果三个月试用期进展顺利,你将获得为期一年的Z签证和工作许可。

卓越的职业发展道路:通过职业发展计划,该职位为那些有志者提供一条通向销售管理职位的快速路径。欢迎申请者向我们的人力资源部门投递完整简历和求职信。

问题参考答案:
① 略。
② 申请者需英语流利且现居上海,或者在获得该职位后能可马上迁到上海。掌握第二外语者优先考虑。申请者需有销售经验,这是其基本职责。

翻译参考答案:
① 申请者需英语流利且现居上海,或者在获得该职位后可马上迁到上海。
② 工资福利很有竞争力,将在面试的时候商谈。

兼职行政助理

公司	DT 集团
身份	兼职雇员
工作	行政助理
行业	职业介绍所
地址	洛杉矶,LA20011
工作性质	行政/文员
履历要求	有工作经验(非管理者)
教育程度	学士学位

职位介绍:招聘兼职工作的高校学生;每天上午工作(大约上午 8:30 到中午 12:00);一家顶尖投资银行中的两个职位空缺;申请者需积极主动、努力工作,具备良好的微软办公软件操作技能,能够在上午工作;硕士生或博士生优先。

工作职责:辅助行政工作;数据录入;文件归档(人工和计算机)

申请条件:本科学历或以上;有办公室工作经验

工资待遇:每小时 17 美元

联系方式:公司:DT 集团;电子邮件:ABC@dt-la.com;职位编号:ABC-PTEE

翻译参考答案:
① 申请者需积极主动、努力工作,具备良好的微软办公软件操作技能,能够在上午工作
② 辅助行政工作
③ 文件归档(人工和计算机)

④ 有办公室工作经验

北京公寓出租

新两居,可自己做饭,位于北京市中心地带,靠近天安门广场、天坛、地铁5号线和2号线。两卧,1个卫生间,可住四到五人。价格:每天40到100英镑。

假期出租:全新住宅楼,位于北京中心地带,紧邻天安门广场、天坛、地铁2号线崇文门站、地铁5号线磁器口站。全新精装,设备一流,家具电器齐全。总之,如果你想在这座美好的古城寻找住处,不需要再四处寻找,请邮件联系我:zbjzf@gmail.com。

周边活动场所:儿童游乐场、电影院、体育馆、夜总会、饭店、购物、剧院等。

公寓设施:空调、网线、卫星电视、烹饪用具、电梯、加热器、厨房、日用纺织品、微波炉、停车位、冰箱、电视机、洗衣机。

公寓租金:淡季:每天40英镑;旺季:每天100英镑。

翻译参考答案:
① 新两居,可自己做饭
② 全新住宅楼,位于北京市中心地带
③ 设备一流,家具电器齐全

联排(复式)公寓

好了,你总算要安顿下来了。你积累了一点资金,准备扎进房地产市场了。那么,我们来转转吧。

作为美国梦,一个家应该有两个卧室,两个卫生间,一个狗舍,一个车库,两个垃圾桶;应该舒适、安全,并且刚刚在你紧巴巴的预算之内。

不适合你吗?用相同的价格,你可以买20万亩撒哈拉荒地,盖一个别墅,除了你和天空,别无他物,就像没有大海的海滩。

太远了?对了,我明白,你需要大都市的刺激和兴奋。用你这笔钱,你只能买一小块地,可不是这样的房产:舒适并且承受得起,对于像你们这样奋斗中的夫妇,这个不错的二手房就是理想之所。不需要闲逛,它就在你所站的地方。

怎么?感觉有点狭小吗?好,一箭地之外,一桥之隔,熙熙攘攘的大都市之外,有一个有着开阔空间、友好邻居、宽大住所的地方。而且这一切都在你的承受范围之内,让你简直不敢相信有这么好的事情!

问题参考答案:
① 和别的各种现实的或不现实的房子比较,最后突出这所房子的好。
② 略

翻译参考答案：
① 用相同的价格你可以买 20 万亩撒哈拉荒地。
② 舒适并且承受得起，这个不错的二手房是你们这样奋斗中的夫妇的理想之所。

第十二课

早餐菜单

全套早餐 7.5 欧元：四根香肠，两片咸肉，两个鸡蛋，黑白布丁，薯饼，豆类，茶或咖啡，烤面包和黑面包。

小套早餐 5.5 欧元：两根香肠，两片咸肉，一个鸡蛋，黑白布丁，茶或咖啡，烤面包和黑面包。炒鸡蛋（4 个鸡蛋）5 欧元。

问题参考答案：
① 欧式风格早餐（西餐）。
② 略

难忘的海滩读物

《床头忠告》，詹妮弗·威尼著。

这部来自当红作家詹妮弗·威尼的首部作品可能也是所有作品当中最滑稽又最令人心酸的一部。当坎迪斯·夏皮罗得知她的前男友给一家新成立的女性杂志写一个名为"床头忠告"的专栏的时候，她感到受到了侮辱。坎尼的担心和烦恼——体重问题、男人问题、工作问题，这些都太逼真了。千万不要错过这位天才作家的首部小说，它将让你捧腹大笑的同时去拿手帕（擦眼泪）。

问题参考答案：
① 让人大笑又让人流泪。
② 略

翻译参考答案：
① 这可能是所有作品当中最滑稽又最令人心酸的一部。
② 她的担心和烦恼——体重问题、男人问题、工作问题，这些都太逼真了。
③ 它将让你捧腹大笑的同时去拿手帕（擦眼泪）。

中国重要摇滚歌手：崔健

生于 1961 年的崔健在他二十出头的时候开始迷恋西方的摇滚。他有着旺盛的创造力和激情，不断地尝试新的风格。从朋克、爵士、非洲音乐到说唱风格，都可以在他的音乐中找到影子，给这种特别的崔氏风格增添了感染力和力量。2002

年,崔健组织并参演了"云南丽江雪山音乐节"——被称为"中国的伍德斯托克音乐节"。这是世界上海拔最高的音乐节。那年的下半年崔健发起了"真唱运动",在全国各高校和其他会场召开了一系列的音乐研讨会,旨在唤醒公众对中国娱乐圈暗暗滋生蔓延的假唱的认识。

问题参考答案:
① 融合了各种西方流行的摇滚风格。
② "云南丽江雪山音乐节"和"真唱运动"。

翻译参考答案:
① 生于1961年
② 从朋克、爵士、非洲音乐到说唱风格,都可以在他的音乐中找到影子。
③ 崔健组织并参演了"云南丽江雪山音乐节"。

中国时装品牌进军纽约时尚界

在很多西方人眼中,中国的时装似乎还仅仅停留在旗袍和毛式服装的阶段。然而这一印象被一场在纽约的时装秀改变了。这场时装秀是由卡宾带来的,它是中国的一个著名的男装品牌,目前正计划进军全球市场。这场时装秀标志着第一次有中国内地的服装设计师参加纽约时装周。

35岁的设计师卡宾所带来的展品以水洗牛仔、"古董"T恤、个性化上装和时尚运动鞋——在纽约、米兰、伦敦以及卡宾所在的广州,这些都是当代男士休闲装的主要流行元素——为特色。

翻译参考答案:
35岁的设计师卡宾的展品以水洗牛仔、"古董"T恤、个性化上装和时尚运动鞋——在纽约、米兰、伦敦以及卡宾所在的广州,这些都是当代男士休闲装的主要流行元素——为特色。

北京的酒吧

北京的夜晚和白天一样繁忙而充满生气。从传统的京剧到浮华的迪斯科,从简陋的酒馆到优雅讲究的酒吧,从茶馆到朋克摇滚俱乐部,无论品位如何,你都一定能在北京找到吸引你的地方。

北京的酒吧场所不断发展,不过三里屯酒吧街是这一切的源头,而且依然比其他区域吸引着更多的在周末刷夜找乐的人。从老牌的"树"到新冒出来的"中国娃娃",三里屯总是可以有一些东西吸引着你。不远处是工人体育馆区域("工体"),那里的"面孔""维克"和"娃娃脸"三家酒吧是最受欢迎的。富有一点的人群会选择CBD街道上的"中心""澜"或者"咏叹调"。几年前还荒凉的后海湖区,现在以它的酒吧数量和种类足以与三里屯相匹敌,而且后海有更好的景色。

不妨去去"东岸爵士俱乐部""天使湾",或者这个区域前卫并且是北京最美的酒吧之一的"未名"。在西北部,海淀五道口的学生氛围使得它并不那么炫目,但是附近也有一些很好的娱乐场所:"拉什"白天黑夜都很热闹,"D-22"是北京最好的音乐酒吧之一。(其他这类的竞争者还有"愚公移山""Mao Livehouse"和"石舟"等。)

问题参考答案:
① 北京的酒吧有各种各样的特色,不同的区域适合各种不同的人群。
② 略

翻译参考答案:
① 无论品位如何,你都一定能在北京找到吸引你的地方。
② 五道口区域的学生氛围使得它并不那么炫目,但是附近也有一些很好的娱乐场所。

名言警句

纸包不住火

英雄所见略同

欲速则不达

有钱能使鬼推磨

骑墙(脚踩两只船)

爱屋及乌

入乡随俗

画蛇添足

半斤八两

开门见山

好事多磨

附录3:翻译练习
Appendix III: Translation Exercises

Exercise One

1. 把下面的句子译成汉语
   a. Be a problem-solver.

   b. Tea may be the most commonly consumed drink on the planet.

   c. This is a gripping, moving novel about family and loyalty by this young writer.

   d. She has been blessed with success, beauty, and, most important, a happy family.

   e. True they have not affected our history and literature as those of Greece and Rome have done, but they will be found rich in interest and instruction.

2. 说明下面的译句所使用的翻译方法
   a. The boat sank off the coast.
      船在离海岸不远处沉没了。(   )
   b. It is well known that the earth is round.
      大家都知道地球是圆的。(   )
   c. to protect brain from the effects of ageing
      保护大脑,使其不受衰老的影响。(   )
   d. Women use dishonesty to avoid conflict.
      女人撒谎为的是避免冲突。(   )
   e. Although they are poor, they are happy.
      他们虽然很穷,但是很快乐。(   )

3. 指出并改正下面译句中的错误
   a. I forgot my key in the car.
      我忘了钥匙在车里。

   b. Each area is identified by a keyword.
      每个领域被代表一个关键词。

   c. He shoots one of them dead.
      他开枪杀他们中的一个死了。

   d. Don't obsess over things.
      别困扰那些事情。

   e. (...which) were often received by the West with no clear idea of where they had originated.
      西方人接受了不知道哪里它们来的。

4. 为画线词语选择合适的对应词
   a. Shut out negative noise and go for it.
      _____ 消极的声音,一心一意去做。(关闭,除掉,排除)

   b. The technical inventions of course traveled faster and further than the scientific thought.
      技术发明当然比科学思想_____更快、更远。(发展得,旅行得,传播得)

   c. You can begin to tap into the health benefits of exercise through many forms of physical activity.
      通过各种形式的身体活动,你可以逐渐_____锻炼给健康带来的益处。(接到,得到,找到)

   d. You may not lower your cholesterol or trim your waistline in a few weeks.
      这或许不会__1__你的胆固醇,或者让你的腰围__2__。(1. 减低,降低,低下;2. 成小,长小,缩小)

   e. A new study reveals how substances found in tea may help prime the body's immune system to fight off infection.
      一项新的研究揭示了茶叶中发现的物质是__1__增强免疫系统,__2__

_____抵抗疾病传染的。(1. 如此,为何,如何；2. 为了,从而,所以)

Exercise Two

1. 把下面的句子译成汉语

   a. A language broadens your choice of career.

   b. More than 382,000 people are treated for skin cancer each year in Australia.

   c. Sometimes you need to lay back and smell the roses.

   d. Would you like it gift-wrapped?

   e. Even within Europe, the survey brought out considerable differences in what women hoped to get from their work.

2. 说明下面的译句所使用的翻译方法

   a. You learn things that you would otherwise never come across.
      你会学到很多东西,而这些东西是用别的方式不可能学到的。(   )

   b. at least 60 to 90 minutes a day may be needed (to maintain weight loss)
      (要保持减轻重量,)一天至少需要60到90分钟的运动。(   )

   c. Let the facts speak for themselves.
      让事实说话。(   )

   d. 15 minutes for regular processing and 10 minutes for expedited processing (a sign in the passport office).
      常规处理15分钟,加急处理10分钟。(   )

   e. There was something original, independent, and heroic about the plan that pleased all of them.
      那个方案有创意,别出心裁,也很大气,所以人人都喜欢。(   )

3. 指出并改正下面译句中的错误

   a. He is better, though not yet cured.
      他更好了,不过还没痊愈。

   b. This pair of shoes fit me better.
      这双鞋子合我的脚好一点。

c. She was 23 and newly married, a law student about to start a summer job.
她是一个 23 岁的法律专业学生而刚刚结婚,正要开始做一份暑假工作。

d. This wish was strongest in Bombay and weakest in Japan.
这种愿望在孟买最强而且在日本最弱。

e. Like the EU, China also has a strong demand to meet its energy-saving objectives.
好像欧盟一样,中国也有满足节能目标的重大要求。

4. 为画线词语选择合适的对应词

a. It led, however, to the formation of a 'Language Institution' in London.
这_____促成了一所语言学校在伦敦的成立。(可,却,便)

b. What's so hard about staying home to take care of two young children?
待在家里照看两个小孩_____有什么难的?(毕竟,究竟,竟然)

c. Plurilinguals as a group think in more flexible and divergent ways than monolinguals as a group.
_____单一语言人群_____,多语人群思考问题更灵活、更多样化。(比……起来;与……相比;比……来说)

d. You have no way of knowing whether a lupu might be a bear trap, a poisonous snake, an armed robber or a starving wolf.
你绝不可能猜出"lupu"_____是捕熊的陷阱、一条毒蛇、一个武装劫匪,_____一条饿狼。(或者……或者;不……而是;究竟……还是)

e. Despite vast economic interchange between China and the United States, cultural insight into Chinese society remains limited.
_____中美之间有大量的经济交流,_____我们对中国社会在文化方面的深入了解仍然很有限。(即使……还是……,不管……却……,虽然……但是……)

Exercise Three

1. 说明下面的译句所使用的翻译方法

a. There is not an iota of truth in his story.
他的故事全是假的。(　　　　)

b. But sometime during the fifth year, the bamboo tree grows about 90 feet in six weeks.

但是在第五年的某个时候，竹子在六个星期里长高了90英尺。（   ）

c. We used to have a touch football game called the "Geller Bowl".

我们过去有一种触身式橄榄球比赛，叫作"杰乐杯赛"。（   ）

d. As a newcomer, she's ignorant of the situation of our company.

她是个新人，对我们公司的情况完全不了解。（   ）

e. After you start getting tired, you start getting cold, you start sweating-those are the types of things that lower your body temperature.

当你开始感到疲劳以后，你就开始觉得冷了，而且开始出汗——就是这些降低了你的体温。（   ）

f. When I got off the plane, the first thing I saw was my family, excitedly waving posters printed with a strange message.

下飞机以后，我首先看到的是我的家人，他们兴奋地挥舞着标语，那上面印了一句奇怪的话。（   ）

g. Each time I came across a character I did not know, I scribbled it down on my palm, transferring it later to a flash card, which I would review throughout the day when I found myself waiting in lines.

每次遇到不认识的字时，我都要把它记在手掌上，然后把它誊在一张卡片上，平时排队时我就可以复习了。（   ）

h. Much of the common ground could be found in the ideas about good health and having good human relationships on the whole and positive ones within the family.

大多数共同点存在于对身体健康、总体上拥有良好的人际关系以及积极的家庭关系的看法上。（   ）

2. 指出并改正下面译句中的错误

   a. Women feel they have to be nice.

   女性觉得她们一定要好。

   b. In despite of the weather, they decided to go.

   虽然是天气，他们还是决定去。

   c. It is offensive to make such comparison.

   这是令人不快的来这样比较。

d. He supposedly cannot talk back, but often Jon seems to be able to tell what he is saying.

不管加菲猫好像不会回话,但是约翰平常能明白它的意思。

e. Even if more time had been available, this company would not have finished that project.

即使更多的时间可以得到,这家公司也不可能完成这个工程。

f. Readers joined some authors in a plea to J.K. Rowling not to kill off Harry Potter in the seventh and final book.

读者也一些作家联合请求J.K.罗琳不要在第七部,也就是最后一部书中杀死哈利·波特。

g. The society was bound together by social principles of great strength and virtue.

这个社会被具有强大力量和道德标准的社会原则结合在一起。

h. But much less interest has been shown here at home in the Chinese language and literature than either of those countries.

但是在国内,对于中国语言文学所表现的兴趣,比较那两个国家来要少得多。

3. 翻译短文

The Maya pyramids were chosen by our panel of experts as one of the seven New Wonders of the World not only for their magnificent physical presence at excavated sites such as Chichen Itza, Uxmal and Tulum on Mexico's Yucatan Peninsula, Tikal in Guatemala, Copan in Honduras and Lamanai in Belize but also for the intellectual achievements of the people.

Exercise Four

1. 说明下面的译句所使的翻译方法
   a. Insist on being well paid.
      坚持要求较高的薪水。(   )
   b. Women use dishonesty to avoid conflict.
      女人撒谎为的是避免冲突。(   )
   c. The team is yet to win a game.
      这支球队还没赢过一场比赛。(   )
   d. If you see benefits—and most people do…
      假如你看到了好处,而大多数人也看到了好处。(   )
   e. Although they are poor, they are happy.
      他们虽然很穷,但是很快乐。(   )
   f. It is not possible but that there should be lessons of the mankind.
      这里肯定有人类应该学习的经验。(   )
   g. Then she found an Internet firm that tracks down hard-to-find people for a small fee.
      后来她发现了一家网络公司,这家公司追踪难以找到的人,费用很低。(   )
   h. A new research has identified more than 700 reasons to study languages.
      一项新的研究发现,学习外语的原因多达700多种。(   )

2. 指出并改正下面译句中的错误
   a. After graduation they lost touch.
      毕业后他们丢了联系。

   b. Women tend to wait for an opportunity to present itself.
      女人倾向于等着为机会到来。

   c. Walking is often underrated as a form of exercise.
      散步常常被低估成一种运动。

   d. We are talking about my future.
      我们在谈论关于我的未来。

   e. Human rights activists have been angered by the argument that moral compromise is the cost of doing big business.

人权主义者被恼火因为有人说道德妥协是做大生意的代价。

f. The book begins, for example, not in China, but in Dortmund.
这本书开始,例如,不是在中国,而是在多特蒙德。

g. EU maintains high-standards and efficient technologies in construction, transport and industry.
欧盟保持着高标准和有效的技术在建筑、运输和工业方面。

h. If this means doctors are able to detect skin cancer early then we are talking about life-saving technology.
如果这项技术的意思是医生能够较早发现皮肤癌,就我们是在谈论一种节省生命的技术。

3. 翻译短文

a. Robert De Niro directs Eric Roths intriguing screenplay about the origins of the CIA, but he lacks the storytelling abilities of the best filmmakers. Matt Dillon and Angelina Jolie offer star power but the characters they play are cold and distancing. On the plus side, an excellent supporting cast is employed and there are some fine, disturbing sequences.

b. She is at a crossroads. Her marriage is not what it should be and her daughter is all grown up. When she survives a terrible boating accident off the coast of Maine, it's time to reassess her life, her love, herself and find out what comes after the moment that changes everything.

附录 4：翻译练习参考答案
Appendix IV: Keys to the Translation Exercises

Exercise One

1. a. 做一个解决问题的人。
   b. 茶可能是世界上消费最广泛的饮料。
   c. 这是这位年轻作家所写的关于家庭和忠诚的一部引人入胜、令人感动的小说。
   d. 她有幸拥有成功和美丽——最重要的是，拥有一个幸福的家庭。
   e. 它们的确不像希腊和罗马文明那样影响过我们的历史和文学，但是不难发现它们在趣味和教育意义上是很丰富的。
2. a. 反译   b. 转译   c. 分译   d. 转译   e. 增译
3. a. 我把钥匙忘在车里了。
   b. 每个领域由一个关键词代表。
   c. 他开枪打死了他们中的一个。
   d. 别让那些事情困扰你。
   e. 西方人接受了它们，却不知道它们的来源。
4. a. 排除   b. 传播得   c. 得到   d. 降低；缩小   e. 如何；从而

Exercise Two

1. a. 掌握一门外语可以扩大你的职业选择。
   b. 澳大利亚每年有超过 382,000 人因皮肤癌接受治疗。
   c. 有时你需要放松一下，享受生活。
   d. 您需要把礼物包装一下吗？
   e. 调查显示，即使在欧洲，妇女希望从工作中得到的东西也有很大不同。
2. a. 分译   b. 转译   c. 省译   d. 分译   e. 分译
3. a. 他虽然还没痊愈，但是好多了。
   b. 这双鞋子更合我的脚。
   c. 她是一个 23 岁、刚刚结婚的法律专业学生，正要开始做一份暑假工作。

d. 这种愿望在孟买最强而在日本最弱。

e. 像欧盟一样,中国也有满足节能目标的重大需求。

4. a. 却　　b. 究竟　　c. 与……相比　　d. 究竟……还是

e. 虽然……但是……

Exercise Three

1. a. 反译　　b. 倒译　　c. 分译　　d. 反译　　e. 转译

f. 分译、增译　　g. 倒译、省译　　h. 转译

2. a. 女性觉得她们一定要友善。

b. 虽然天气不太好,他们还是决定去。

c. 这样的比较是令人不快的。

d. 尽管加菲猫好像不会回话,但是约翰通常能明白它的意思。

e. 即使有更多的时间,这家公司也不可能完成这个工程。

f. 读者和一些作家联合请求J.K.罗琳不要在第七部,也就是最后一部书中杀死哈利·波特。

g. 这个社会由具有强大力量的社会原则和美德结合在一起。

h. 但是在国内,对于中国语言文学所表现的兴趣,比起那两个国家来要小得多。

3. 玛雅金字塔之所以被专家小组选为世界新七大奇迹之一,不仅因为它们在诸如墨西哥半岛上的齐辰伊贾、尤克斯莫尔、土兰、瓜太玛拉的蒂卡尔、洪都拉斯的科潘、伯利兹的拉玛来等地的发掘现场所表现出来的宏伟的外观,而且因为它们体现了原住民的杰出智慧。

Exercise Four

1. a. 转译　　b. 转译　　c. 反译　　d. 增译　　e. 增译

f. 反译　　g. 分译、转译　　h. 分译、增译

2. a. 毕业后他们失去了联系。

b. 女人倾向于等待机会自己到来。

c. 散步作为一种运动常常被低估了。

d. 我们在谈论我的未来。

e. 人权主义者被激怒了,因为有人说道德妥协是做大生意的代价。

f. 例如,这本书不是从中国,而是从多特蒙德开始。

g. 欧盟在建筑、运输和工业方面保持着很高的标准和高效的技术。

h. 如果这项技术意味着医生能够较早发现皮肤癌,那我们就是在谈论一种拯救生命的技术。

3. a. 罗伯特·德尼罗是厄里克·罗斯关于中央情报局起源的引人入胜的剧本的导演,不过他缺少优秀电影制作者那种讲故事的能力。迈特·狄龙和安吉丽娜·朱莉表现了巨星的能量,不过他们表演的角色显得冷漠而有距离感。从好的方面看,除了主角外,剧组的其他演员阵容相当出色,电影里也有一些细致的、富于变化的情节。

b. 她正处在十字路口。她的婚姻不太如意,女儿已经长大成人。经历了缅因州海岸边可怕的轮船事故并幸存下来后,该是她重新评估一下生活、爱情、自身以及那个改变一切的瞬间之后发生的事情的时候了。

附录5:译作选登
Appendix V: Selected Sample Translation Papers

为什么学中文——理雅各就职演说
Inaugural Lecture

James Legge, October 27, 1876, Oxford

Eight years ago Professor Müller commenced his inaugural lecture in the Chair of Comparative Philology with this sentence: —'The foundation of a professorial Chair in the University of Oxford marks an important epoch in the history of every new science.' The sentiment and words appear to me appropriate in entering on the duties of my own appointment to the recently constituted Chair of the Chinese Language and Literature.

This is not, indeed, the first Chinese Chair that has been constituted in England. I commenced the study of the language towards the end of 1838, under the Rev. Samuel Kidd, in London University College. The first Englishman that distinguished himself by his attainments in Chinese was the Rev. Dr. Robert Morrison, who went from this country as the first Protestant Missionary to China in 1807, and was the pioneer of English-speaking Sinologists.

Dr. Morrison being in England in 1825, the introduction of the study of Chinese into one or both of the University of Oxford and Cambridge, was agitated by him. This earliest attempt to have the claims of Chinese recognized in this country failed. It led, however, to the formation of a 'Language Institution' in London, where Dr. Morrison taught Chinese for several months to a class of thirteen students. After his death in 1834, a committee purchased his Chinese library and made it over to the London University College, on condition that the Council should constitute a professorship of the Chinese Language and Literature. This was the Chair that was filled by the Rev. Samuel Kidd, who was well qualified for the position.

Even if Dr. Morrison had obtained the establishment of a Chair in Oxford or Cambridge in 1825, England would have been forestalled by France in the encouragement of Chinese studies. In 1814 a Chinese professorship was constituted in the College of France and conferred on Etienne Fourmont, —of all men then in Europe, out of Russia, the best qualified for such a Chair. Contemporaneously with the constitution of the Chair in University College, London, in 1838, a Chair of Chinese was established in the University of Berlin. Chinese Chairs of later constitution also exist at München and Vienna. At Leyden in Holland, since 1850, Professor Hoffmann has given instruction in Japanese, and also in Chinese as subsidiary to that; and with him there has been associated of late years Professor Schlegel, specially to prepare young men by a knowledge of Chinese for service as interpreters in the Dutch East Indias. Since 1864 the Italian Government has promoted the study of both Chinese and Japanese in Florence.

八年前,穆勒教授用这样的句子开始他的比较语文学教席的就职演说:"在牛津大学,设立一个教授席位,也就开始了那个学科历史上的一个重要时代。"当我自己开始履行刚刚设立的中国语言文学教席职责的时候,这种感情和语言对我来说是再适合不过了。

这当然不是英国设立的第一个中文教席。我于1838年底在伦敦大学的萨穆尔·修德教士的指导下开始学习中文。第一个以中文的成就闻名于世的英国人是教士罗伯特·马礼逊博士,他于1807年作为第一个新教传教士去了中国,是说英语的汉学家中的先驱。

1825年马礼逊博士回英国,他积极鼓动,想在牛津、剑桥,或是两所大学中的一所引进中文。要求在英国承认中文的最初尝试虽然失败了,但是,这促成了一所语言学校在伦敦的成立;在那里,马礼逊教一个班13个学生中文,教了几个月。他1834年去世后,一个委员会买下了他的中文图书馆,并把它转交给伦敦大学学院,条件是大学理事会设立一个中国语言文学教席。这就是由萨穆尔·修德担任的那个教席,他对于这个职位是非常胜任的。

即便是1825年马礼逊博士得到了在牛津或剑桥开展中文教学的机会,在鼓励中文学习方面英国也还是落后于法国。1814法国就在法兰西学院设立了中文教授席位,并把它授予了傅尔蒙——除了俄国之外,当时欧洲最胜任这样一个职位的人。就在1838年伦敦大学学院设立中文教席的同时,柏林大学也设立了一个中文教席。此后慕尼黑、维也纳也设立了这样的教席。在荷兰莱顿,从1850年起,霍夫曼教授就开始教授日语和作为辅修课的汉语;在后来的几年中,由施勒格尔教授协助,专门给年轻学生讲授中文知识,以备担任荷属东印度公司的翻译。从1864年开始,意大利政府开始在佛罗伦萨推广中文和日语学习。

  To complete our review to what has been done in Europe for the cultivation of Chinese studies, it only remains for me to go with you for a minute or two to Russia. In 1685, a number of Russian soldiers, with one or more priests, had been carried from Albazin to Peking, where they were well treated, being allowed the exercise of their religion, while the soldiers were received into the emperor's body-guard. On the death of the religious instructors the sovereign, known to us as K'ang-hi, a really great man, requested that others might be sent from Russia to supply their place. Thus originated, in 1715, a Russian Mission in the capital of China. Several of the Russians at Peking have been men of great linguistic ability and research. They have translated important Chinese books, and published original Works on China and the northern regions of Asia; —many of them of the greatest value.

  I have thus given a brief sketch of what has been done in Europe up to the present time for the promotion of Chinese studies. During the last sixty years English sinologists in China have not been in the rear of those of France or Russia, but much less interest has been shown here at home in the Chinese language and literature than either of those countries. The time has come for Great Britain to occupy in this respect a new position, and I am pleased to think that the constitution of the Chinese Chair here will contribute to hasten on this better state of things, which is now required by our relations with China, political, religious, and commercial, —all of them very different from what they were forty years ago.

  Politically, the state of Great Britain in China is not inferior to that of Russia. Within the last four and thirty years, we have entered into no fewer than three treaties with the Chinese Empire. Approaching it by sea on the east, we have now our Legation at Peking; and more than a dozen consulates along its seaboard and the Yangtze River, at each of which the services of a highly qualified interpreter are required.

  I have still to illustrate the point in hand by a reference to the commercial interests of Great Britain in China. This may best be described by the adjective enormous. Our commerce with China is greater than that of all the other nations of Europe together; greater than that of all the rest of the world. For instance, taking the trade returns for last year, 1875, the value of the imports and exports into and out of China was very nearly forty millions of pounds sterling, of which those to and from Great Britain and its foreign possessions amounted to upwards of thirty-one millions and a half, leaving about eight millions and a quarter to be distributed between eleven other treaty and sundry non-treaty Powers. Again, in the tables compiled by order of the Inspector-General of Chinese maritime customs for the Universal Exhibition at Vienna in 1873, I find that, on the average of the three years 1870, 71, 72, the value of the gross total of commodities, both foreign and native, that arrived at or left all treaty ports, re-exports being included, is put down at between 115 and 116 millions of pounds, of which the proportion conveyed by British shipping was over sixty millions of pounds, or more than one-half of the whole.

我们对欧洲在促进中文学习方面所做工作的回顾，现在只剩下了俄国。我要跟你们一道，用一两分钟来看看俄国的情况。1685年，一些俄国士兵以及一位或几位牧师，被从阿尔巴赞送到北京。在北京，他们受到了款待，并被允许开展宗教活动。士兵们被吸收进皇家卫队。教士去世的时候，皇帝——也就是我们知道的康熙——一个真正了不起的人，请求俄国派其他的人来补充教士的职位。这就使得1715年在中国的首都出现了一个俄国使团。其中一些人具有出色的语言天赋和研究能力。他们翻译了一些重要的中文书籍，并且出版了一些关于中国以及亚洲北部地区的著作——其中不少具有重要价值。

我刚才概括地介绍了到目前为止欧洲在促进中国研究方面所做的工作。在过去的六十年里，英国在华汉学家并没有落在法国的或俄国的汉学家之后。然而，在（英国）国内，对于中国语言文学所显示的兴趣，比起这两个国家来说，要少得多。英国在这个方面占据一个新的位置的时代已经到来。我非常乐观地认为，中文教席的设立，将有助于加快我们这种有利状态的发展，而这正是目前我们与中国的政治、宗教、商业关系所需要的，所有这些方面都与四十年前截然不同了。从政治上说，英国在华势力不弱于俄国。在过去的三十四年内，我们已经与中国签订了至少三个条约。我们从东方的海上进入中国，目前已经在北京设立了使团，在它的沿海、沿江建立了十几个领事馆，每一处领事馆都需要高质量的翻译。

我还要引用英国在华商业利益的例证，来说明我们的观点。我们的利益完全可以用"巨大"来形容。我们与中国的商贸，比欧洲其他国家加在一起还要庞大，比世界其他国家加在一起还要庞大。以去年——1875年的贸易利润为例，中国的进出口总值接近四千万英镑。其中与英国及其海外领地的贸易额总计高达三千一百五十万；剩下大约八百二十五万由十一个条约国及其他各类非条约国分配。此外,在中国海关总长为1873年维也纳世界博览会下令编写的表格里,我发现,在1870、1871、1872三年时间里,到达和离开所有开放港口(通商口岸)的日用商品——包括外国的和本地的,包括再次出口的,记录的总值年均在一亿一千五百万到一亿一千六百万英镑之间,其中由英国商船运送的超过六千万英镑,或者说超过总值的一半以上。

  My idea of a great university is that it is a great institution for the promotion of learning and education. To the country in which it is established it owes the duty of imparting to its youth the highest knowledge which the age enjoys on all subjects belonging to the culture of the mind and the formation of the character. Now the number and range of subjects embraced in the field of study must increase from age to age, to keep pace with the researches of science and the results of various investigations. Science in connexion with China I will not speak, but its history and literature ought no longer to be excluded from a scheme of university education. True they have not affected our history and literature as those of Greece and Rome have done, but they will be found rich in interest and instruction. There in the south-eastern corner of Asia the people had existed for thousands of years, little more than known by name to the nations which were acting the great drama of history in the West, —acting it in earnest, and not in show or play. As Virgil, towards the dawn of our Christian era, spoke of the Britons as entirely divided from the east of the world, so a writer might have written of the Chinese three centuries ago. And yet they had had their local habitation and name from the remote date which I have indicated, existing in a state of high civilization, with a very various literature, bound together by social principles of great strength and virtue, and having increased till their number was double the population of the great Roman empire in its palmist days. It is not possible but that there should be lessons of the mankind.

  There is now little difficulty or uncertainty in the interpretation of the most ancient Chinese documents. How a language without inflexions can be understood so readily, may appear strange; but Chinese has its own laws; and as Julien, in the latest work which came from his pen, observes: —"It answers well enough to all the requirements of thought to have allowed Chinese writers, for more than twenty centuries, and in innumerable Works, to treat all the subjects, scientific or literary, that exercise the human spirit". Indeed the meaning of the writer in good Chinese composition strikes the mind as forcibly as the most eloquent sentences of an alphabetic language, —being a thing seen weightier than a thing heard. Nor is the spoken language an inadequate vehicle of discourse. I have seen the statement that it is impossible to conceive of a Chinese Parliament or Debating Society; but I have listened to triumphs of oratory in China as great as ever I have known in this country.

  我对一所伟大的大学的看法,它是一个推广知识和教育的伟大的机构。对于建立它的国家,它负有向这个国家的青年传授最崇高的知识的责任,这些知识是这个时代享有的,属于思想文化、性格形成的所有学科的知识。现在,为了与科学研究和各种考察的结果同步发展,包含在研究领域的学科的数量和范围应该是随着时代而增长的。我不讨论与中国有关的科学领域,但是,中国的历史和文学,决不应再被排斥在大学教育的计划之外了。的确,它们没有像希腊和罗马的历史和文学那样影响过我们;但是,我们会发现,它们在趣味和教育意义上是丰富的。在亚洲东南角,那里的人民已经存在了好几千年,不管是实质上还是表面上,他们有着波澜壮阔的历史,但西方对他们知之甚少。按照基督纪元黎明时期的维吉尔所说,英国从世界的东方整个分离出来,所以某位作家很可能三个世纪前就已经写到了中国人。然而从我前面提到的遥远的时代起,他们就已经有了自己的居所和姓氏,在一种高度文明的状态下生活,拥有丰富多样的文学作品,由具有强大力量的社会原则和美德联结在一起;并且他们的人口不断增长,直至其最为繁荣的时期,人口达到伟大的罗马帝国的两倍。这里面肯定包含了人类应该学习的东西。

  目前,在绝大部分中国古代典籍的理解上已经不存在太多困难或者疑惑。一种没有形态变化的语言怎么能如此容易理解呢?这看似奇怪,其实中文有自己的语法。就像儒莲在其最近的著作中所做的观察:它满足表达思想所需的各种条件,所以两千多年来的中国作家在浩如烟海的著作中能够进行激励人类精神的各种讨论——无论是科学还是文学方面。的确,在中文的经典著作里,作者的思想对于我们心灵撞击的程度与字母语言最意味深长的语句相比毫不逊色。眼见为实,汉语的口语也足以担当交流的工具。我曾经见过这样的论断,说在中国设立议会或议院是难以想象的。但是我在中国听到过的演讲,与我在自己的国家听到过的演讲一样雄辩。

I have thus endeavoured to give you some of the reasons for the constituting of a Chinese Chair at Oxford; reasons springing from our relations with China, political, religion, and commercial, and reasons springing from the functions of a university in the pursuit of truth and the work of education.

I would almost venture to hope that the event may find a response even in China itself. The most satisfactory proof that the Chinese Government is waking from the sleep and bursting the shackles of ages, and rousing itself to put an end to the national isolation, is afforded by the fact that there are now about a hundred young men sent by it in the United States, to remain there for fifteen years, first to acquire the English language, then to learn various sciences and professions, and finally to return to China and be employed in the public service as the government shall direct. I made the voyage with the first instalment of those lads from China to San Francisco in 1873, and know well the Chinese gentlemen who have been the chief promoters of the scheme. I would fain hope that as a result from the appointment of this Chair, and the interest thereby shown to be cherished in their country and language, some of the leading minds in China may be stirred to promote the sending to England, as well as to the United States, companies of their young countrymen, to prosecute, here or elsewhere, general studies, and then to return and diffuse the knowledge which they have acquired, using their influence also to maintain sentiments of friendship between their own country and Great Britain. So shall the Chair prove, not merely, in the words of my opening sentence, an important epoch in the history of the science of language, but also an important auxiliary to the maintenance of peace, and a good understanding between two great nations.

以上我试图解释为何要在牛津大学设立中文教席；原因既包括我们与中国的政治、宗教和商业关系，也包括一所大学在追求真理和开展教育上应有的作用。

我甚至大胆地希望，这一事件在中国也能得到一个回应。中国政府正在从沉睡中醒来，挣脱时代的枷锁，奋起摆脱国家的孤立状态；最好的证明就是最近有大约一百名年轻学生被派到美国。他们要待在那里15年，先是学会英语，然后进行各种学科和专业的学习，最后返回中国，由政府指派在公共部门服务。1873年，我同那些首批去学习的年轻人在同一条船上航行去旧金山，并且了解了推动这一计划的几位中国绅士。我乐观地希望，这个教席的设立，以及由此显示的对他们国家和语言的重视，将会激起中国的一些有影响的人除了向美国派遣学生外，也推动向英国派遣留学生；成群的中国年轻人在这里以及其他地方开展广泛的学习，然后返回中国传播学到的知识，同时用他们的影响来维持中英之间的友好感情。因此，这个教席将会证明——它不仅仅标志着在我的就职演讲中所说的语言科学发展的重要时代的到来，而且也是在两个国家之间维持和平、达成理解的重要辅助手段。

(Inaugural lecture on the constituting of a Chinese chair in the University of Oxford, delivered in the Sheldonian Theatre, October 27, 1876, by Rev. James

Legge, Professor of the Chinese Language and Literature.)

（本文是理雅各就任牛津大学中国语言文学教授席位的演说。在演说中，他回顾了欧洲"汉学"的发展历史，介绍了中国语言文学的特点和成就，从政治、经济、文化等方面阐述了开展中国语言文学教学和研究的必要性。）

理雅各（James Legge, 1815—1897），英国汉学家，以翻译中国儒家、道家经典而闻名于世。1843—1873年在华传教，1876年起任牛津大学中国语言文学教授，直至去世。
Müller(F. Max Müller)：麦克思·穆勒（1823—1900），德裔英国语文学家、东方学家。
Rev. Samuel Kidd：修德教士（1804—1843），英国汉学家，伦敦大学首任中文教授。
Rev. Dr. Robert Morrison：马礼逊教士/博士（1782—1843），英国汉学家，伦敦布道会教士。
Etienne Fourmont：傅尔蒙（1683—1745），法国汉学家，法兰西学院教授，主讲阿拉伯语。
Hoffmann：霍夫曼（Johann Hoffmann, 1851—1878），德国汉学家。
Schlegel：施古德（1840—1903），荷兰汉学家，莱顿大学首任中文教授。
Virgil：维吉尔（B.C. 70—19），古罗马诗人。
Julien：儒莲（Stanislas A. Julien, 1797—1873），法国汉学家。

我在中国的生活
My Life in China

Ian McMorran

It is no exaggeration to say that when I came to live in China about two and a half years ago it was to realize a life-long dream. After two and a half years, I can say that my life in China has brought me quite a few surprises, including a few unpleasant ones, but I have not been disappointed. On the contrary, I have been happier than I could possibly have expected, and shall almost certainly stay here for the foreseeable future, or as long as I am allowed to!

I had always wanted to live in China ever since I began my Chinese studies at Oxford University as an undergraduate back in the nineteen-fifties. In those days the Chinese department at Oxford concentrated on the classical Chinese language and works written in it, so we students read Confucius 孔子, Mencius 孟子, Zhuangzi 庄子, Laozi 老子, the Chunqiu and Zuozhuan 春秋左传, the Shiji 史记, Tangshi sanbaishou 唐诗三百首, and selections of classical prose throughout the history of Imperial China. I was fortunate enough to have as a teacher Wu Shichang 吴世昌 a well-known specialist in 红学. The only modern Chinese we read was Lu Xun's *Madman's Diary* 狂人日记 and an essay by Hu Shi 胡适. Although I and my classmates were keen to learn modern Chinese we had little opportunity.

After graduating, I won a scholarship to study in China, and hoped that, in addition to pursuing my research on the Ming dynasty patriot Wang Chuanshan 王船山(1619—92), I would have the opportunity of learning to speak Putonghua properly, but unfortunately the Cultural Revolution was about to begin in China and I could not get a visa. I was still shut out from the "promised land"! Instead, I went and studied in Hong Kong, Japan, and finally Taiwan, and still remember how I used to listen longingly to radio broadcasts from mainland China, and how the words "北京呼叫!" used to give me goose-pimples.

Years later, when I was teaching Classical Chinese and Chinese intellectual history at Oxford University, I was occasionally invited to China either by the Academy of Social Sciences 社科院 or to take part in Confucian Conferences, but I never stayed for more than a few days at a time. During one such visit, I met my late wife, a girl from Hengyang in Hunan 湖南衡阳(Wang Chuanshan's home-town), but even when visiting her I never stayed long, and she eventually joined me in Europe.

After teaching 25 years at Oxford, I taught for 15 years in Paris, where I was Professor of Chinese Civilization. So it was that when I finally retired from Paris University I came to China. Chinese culture had always been my passion, so the so-called "Professor of Chinese Civilization" finally found himself living in Chinese civilization for the first time-and learning quite a lot about Chinese civilization and culture at first-hand!

大约两年半前来到中国生活的时候,毫不夸张地说,那是圆了我长久以来的一个梦。两年半过去了,可以说这段日子给我带来不少意料不到的体验,包括某些不那么令人愉快的经历;不过,我从未失望。相反地,我比自己所能期待的还要快乐一些;而且,在可以预见的将来,只要条件允许,我多半还会待在这里。

自从20世纪50年代成为牛津大学一名学习中文的本科生以来,我就一直希望来中国生活。那时,牛津大学中文系只教授文言文,我们要读孔子、孟子、庄子、老子、春秋左传、史记、唐诗三百首以及历代散文选。我很幸运,能有吴世昌这样著名的红学家作为老师。我们阅读的现代汉语仅限于鲁迅的《狂人日记》以及胡适的一篇文章。尽管我和我的同学们都非常想学习现代汉语,但是却没有什么机会。

毕业后,我获得了一个到中国学习的奖学金,满心希望着除了从事对明代爱国者王船山(1619—1692)的研究外,还能学好说普通话。不幸的是,中国的"文化大革命"即将开始,我无法拿到签证,被我的"promised land"拒之门外。我转而去了别处学习,先是香港,然后是日本,最后是台湾。我还记得曾经是多么盼望着收听大陆的广播,"北京呼叫"曾经那么令人兴奋。

多年后,当我在牛津大学教授古代汉语和中国思想史时,也曾受到社科院或是别处儒学会议的邀请前往中国,但每次总是逗留不了几天。在其中的一次行程中,我遇见了我目前的妻子,一位来自湖南衡阳(王船山的家乡)的姑娘。不过即便是去看她,也待不了多长时间,而她最终到了欧洲,与我共同生活。

在牛津执教了25年之后,我又在巴黎作为中国文化教授教了15年书。所以,直到从巴黎大学完全退休后,我才终于来到了中国。我对中国文化的热情始终未减,而作为"中国文化教授",我终于平生第一次生活在中国文化之中了——并且亲身体会和学习中华文明和中国文化的许多方面。

It is perhaps ironic that whereas one of my chief motives in coming to China was to perfect my Putonghua, I am actually teaching English at Fudan University and enjoying teaching my own language immensely! I owe this opportunity to one of my graduate students in Paris, a Shanghai girl whose parents acted as my go-betweens with Fudan. I have always been interested in language, and teaching English to Chinese students after so many years teaching Chinese to English and French students has a certain piquancy. Moreover, it is very rewarding-and a lot of fun-working with Chinese students to find the mot juste in English, and of course my knowledge of Chinese helps.

But the way the modern Chinese language has evolved since the time when I started trying to learn it is one of the things that intrigues me more and more since I have been living here. At times, the Putonghua that all young people now speak naturally seems to me like a foreign language! After 2 years, I still find it strange to say and hear "早上好": it seems like an unnatural translation of "Good morning". When I began learning Chinese people just said "早!" That, I feel, is real Chinese. Similarly, the ubiquitous use of the suffix 们 strikes me as the result of too much attention being paid to foreign grammar. Previously, the use of 们 was rather limited. I don't think it figures much in the real Chinese of a writer like Lao She 老舍 or that of his contemporaries. I find 人们 particularly unnecessary: 人家 or 人 used with a recapitulative 都 simply seems more Chinese to me. Perhaps it's a question of generations. All languages are evolving all the time, and people of my generation are not always happy about the changes taking place. In English too, I find myself waging a losing battle against what I consider the improper use of "hopefully", "whether/if", "may/might", "will/shall", "as/like" etc. etc. Of course, we can't prevent these changes, but perhaps our function is to slow them down! Or make younger people aware of what is happening. None of my students realized that the common expression "买单" comes from the Cantonese, for example. I've even been corrected for saying 结账. I hasten to say that I don't speak as an expert, simply as someone who is still struggling to learn what I consider a very beautiful language (both aurally and visually). After all, it's never too late to learn 活到老学到老!

Maybe what I have written above makes me seem very old-fashioned. But on the other hand, one thing that has surprised me about contemporary Chinese culture is how feudal some social relationships still are after more than 50 years of socialism. I am thinking in particular of male-female relationships, and the prevalence of the 男尊女卑 attitude. Of course, as a student of Chinese history I was familiar with such traditional attitudes, but I have been amazed at the extent to which they still survive, both within families and in society at large. To provide details would embarrass friends, but I have personally witnessed situations in which males are accorded privileges and an importance that they are from meriting at the expense of females who are in fact superior to them. Surprisingly enough, most of my students at Fudan seem to accept this as normal. When we discussed a newspaper report of a survey according to which most men wanted to marry women who were shorter, poorer, less well-educated and earned less money than themselves most of the female students accepted this attitude as normal.

有意思的是,虽然我来中国的主要目的是提高普通话水平,但实际上我在复旦大学教起了英语;并且,教授自己的母语给了我极大的快乐。这个机会得益于我在巴黎大学的一名研究生——一位上海姑娘,她的父母是我与复旦大学之间的牵线人。我本来就对语言感兴趣,在教英、法学生这么多年汉语之后,教中国学生英文颇令人感到畅快。与他们一道推敲出英文中最恰当的表达,这本身就充满了乐趣,使人有成就感。我的中文知识也有了用武之地。

不过,自从在这里生活以后,越来越激起我好奇的事情之一,是与我刚开始学习中文时相比,汉语已经发生了一些变化。有时,现在的年轻人自然而然地说出来的普通话,在我听来竟像是一种外语。比如在这里住了两年,当听到"早上好"时,还是觉得别扭。这似乎是 good morning 的一种不太自然的翻译。我开始学汉语的时候,人们只说"早!"我觉得这才是真正的汉语。同样,无处不在的"们"也使我感到外语语法的深刻影响。以前"们"的用法是有限制的。我感觉在像老舍及其同时代人的"真正的"汉语里,"们"并不经常出现。在我看来,"人们"尤其是不必要的;"人家"或是"人"加上表总括的"都"似乎更地道一些。这也许是代沟的问题。所有语言都在变,而像我这一代人并不总是乐于接受改变。英语也是一样。我发现自己发起了一场注定失败的战争,反对那些不正确用法——诸如 hopefully 以及 whether/if、may/might、will/shall、as/like 的误用。当然,我们无法阻止这些变化。我们的作用也许在于让这些变化慢下来,或者让年轻人意识到究竟发生了什么。例如,我的学生没有人注意到常用的"买单"其实来自粤语,我说"结账"的时候还被他们纠正过。我得说我并不是在以专家的身份指手画脚,而只是作为一个仍在艰难地学习一种我认为非常美丽的语言的(无论是听觉上的还是视觉上的)人。毕竟,英文和中文里都有这句话——活到老学到老。

  上面的文字或许使我看起来很古板。然而,我对另一种当代文化现象同样感到吃惊,这就是尽管社会主义实行了50多年,可是在某些社会关系方面居然还是如此封建。我要说的是男女关系,以及男尊女卑观念的盛行。作为学中国历史出身的人,我当然熟悉那些传统思想,但令我吃惊的是在家庭和社会上它们残留的范围如此之广。说出具体的事情可能会令朋友难堪,但我确实目睹过男人们的尊贵是以屈尊女性为代价的,而实际上这些女性要比男人们优秀得多。更令人吃惊的是,我的许多复旦学生似乎认为这可以接受,没什么大不了的。当我们讨论报纸上一篇关于某个社会调查的报道时——根据该调查,男人在择偶时希望"她"比自己矮一些、家庭条件差一些、学历、工资低一些,大部分女生认为理应如此。

  Almost any foreign visitor to China must be struck by the problems created by overpopulation. No matter what one does, it seems that vast numbers of people are doing the same thing at the same time. Of course, this problem is particularly acute when travelling in China, and unfortunately all too often results in a chaotic scramble in which good manners and discipline are lost and a spirit of 争先恐后 reigns. Mainland Chinese are only just beginning to learn to queue, and have some way to go before they catch up with their cousins in Hong Kong, Taiwan or Singapore. Lack of discipline is also a characteristic of behaviour on the roads. Despite the efforts made by the authorities, car-drivers, cyclists, and pedestrians are all too often guilty of breaking the law. I think it is a sad commentary on the traffic situation that one sees posters declaring "以不闯红灯为荣". It ought to be normal, not glorious!

In most respects, however, I must add, I believe that the students I have the privilege of teaching at Fudan are the main reason that I feel extremely optimistic about China's future. Last year, one of my former students from Oxford telephoned me to ask me how I was getting on in China. "I don't want to hurt your feelings," I told him, "But these are the best students I have ever taught." They are not only intelligent, motivated and hard-working. They are also highly civilized. By which I mean that they are considerate to one another, treating each other with respect and friendliness, even though the pressures on young people of their age in China today are considerable, and they are well aware that they are, and will in the future often be, rivals for the best grades, the best scholarships, the best jobs and the best careers. As a visiting French teacher put it, the students here are so "gentils"- so "nice". (Two very French/English words that are difficult to translate into Chinese:良好 seems inadequate, somehow).

Perhaps students at Fudan provide one of the best arguments in favour of elitism, a concept that is almost taboo in both England and France nowadays, where the practice of selection in education has been very much under attack for years (wrongfully, in my opinion).

All in all, I am delighted to be in China, and feel that a new chapter has opened in my own life here, a chapter that coincides with the enormous progress that this country has made since the time when Deng Xiaoping began to institute his policies. In the end, I owe it to him that I can have the life I have in China today.

几乎所有来中国的外国人都会受到由人口过多所带来的问题的困扰。不管你干什么,似乎总有数不清的人同时做着同样的事情。自然,这个问题在旅行时尤为突出,而且常常不幸地发展成为混乱无序的争抢。这时礼貌和纪律荡然无存,一种争先恐后的劲头支配着人们。大陆的人们才刚刚开始学习排队,要赶上他们在中国香港和台湾地区或是新加坡的兄弟姐妹,路还很长。缺乏纪律也表现在道路上。尽管政府付出很多努力,司机、骑车人、步行者违反交通秩序的事情还是屡见不鲜。在这样的场景中,"以不闯红灯为荣"的标语简直就是一句可悲的话。不闯红灯是应该的,谈不上光荣!

不过从很多方面来看,我对中国的未来是非常乐观的;我必须承认我的信心主要来自于我有幸在复旦教的这些学生。去年,我从前的一个牛津的学生打电话来问我在中国过得如何,"我不想让你伤心,"我告诉他,"但是他们的确是我教过的最好的学生。"他们不仅聪明、勤奋好学,而且非常有修养。我指的是他们在乎彼此的感受,相互尊重、友善;尽管今天在他们这个年纪的中国青年压力很大,他们也很清楚在分数、奖学金、工作及职业生涯等方面,他们现在是、将来也会是竞争者。正如一位法国外教所说的,这些同学是如此的文雅、友善("gentils""nice"这两个法语/英语词不容易译成汉语,"良好"似乎还不够贴切)。

也许复旦的学生可以为精英教育提供一个有利的论据。这个概念如今在英国和法国几乎成了一个禁忌,教育领域的优胜劣汰这些年来饱受攻击(我个人认为这些非议是站不住脚的)。

总而言之,我很庆幸来到了中国。我觉得自己的人生翻开了新的一页,而这一页正好与邓小平执政以来中国取得的巨大进步同步展开。最后,我把自己今天能够在中国生活归功于他。

Additions: In terms of language, the simplification of the Chinese script is another area where change has brought problems for me. I was never opposed to it. After all, many of today's simplified forms had existed for centuries, figuring in calligraphy and cursive letter-writing etc. Although not all the new characters are elegant, and I think the Chinese might well have adopted some of the Japanese simplifications already in circulation before China began its reforms (The Japanese simplifications for 传 and 发 are more attractive, for example), my chief quarrel is with modern Chinese dictionaries. Old Chinese dictionaries all shared the same 214 radicals 部首, which were always listed in the same order, thus allowing students like me who seem to have spent their whole lives looking up characters in dictionaries, to memorize their numbers. New dictionaries vary enormously in the number of characters they class as radicals, and in the order in which they are listed. The tendency seems to be heading towards a list of 189 radicals, but the 中华词典, published by 中华书局 in 2000, lists 200, and the Chinese-English Dictionary 汉英词典 published by the Commercial Press 商务印书馆 in 1988, lists 227. (These are a few dictionaries on my bookshelf). Needless to say the radicals are not arranged in the same order. Perhaps the 新华字典 published by the Commercial Press in 2000, and the 汉英词典(修订版) published by 外语教学与研究出版社 in 2001, each with 189 radicals, point the way ahead, but their radicals are not arranged in the same order!

Why this lack of coordination? If simplified characters were designed to make life simpler, why not produce dictionaries for them which are simple to use? Maybe most Chinese look up characters according to their pronunciation, as I do when I know how to pronounce a character, in alphabetical order, directly in the body of the dictionary. But if a radical index is worth having, it ought to be one that is standardized and easy to use. The current state of dictionaries is a mess.

  附:就汉语而言,汉字书写的简化给我带来了另一种困扰。我并不是反对简化字,毕竟今天的很多简化字已经以书法——尤其是草书等形式存在了几个世纪。虽然并非所有新造的字都很优美,并且我认为有些字很可能是来自在中国汉字改革之前就早已在日本使用的简化字(例如日语里对"传""发"的简化就有意思得多),使我感到不习惯的主要是字典。古代的汉语字典使用同样的214个部首,并且按同样的顺序排列,因而就便于像我这样似乎一辈子都在查字典的学生记住部首的数量。新字典在部首的数量、排列的顺序上变化极大,总的趋势似乎是向189个部首发展。但是中华书局2000年出的《中华字典》列了200个部首,而商务印书馆1988年出的《汉—英词典》列出了227个部首。(这些都是我书架上放着的字典)不用说部首的顺序也各不相同。商务印书馆2000年的《新华字典》、外语教学语研究出版社2001年的《汉英词典》(修订版)都只有189个部首,这也许是一个方向。但是其部首的排列顺序又不相同!

  为什么会如此不一致呢?如果简化字是为了让生活更简单,为什么简化字的字典不能做到简便易用呢?也许大多数中国人知道按照音序直接在字典里查一个字——当我知道一个字的读音时也是如此。但是如果一个部首检字目录还值得存在,那它理应是标准化的、便于使用的。目前字典的状况实在是太混乱了。

  *《我在中国的生活》(My life in China)最初发表在《瞭望东方周刊》2007年第10期(总173期)上。作者 Ian McMorran(麦穆伦)教授,曾任教于牛津大学、巴黎第七大学。